Rebel Reporting

John Ross Speaks to Independent Journalists

Edited by Cristalyne Bell and Norman Stockwell

WITH AN INTRODUCTION BY AMY GOODMAN
AND A FOREWORD BY ROBERT W. MCCHESNEY

Hamilton Books

An Imprint of
Rowman & Littlefield
Lanham • Boulder • New York • Toronto • Plymouth, UK

Copyright © 2016 by Hamilton Books
4501 Forbes Boulevard, Suite 200, Lanham, Maryland 20706
Hamilton Books Acquisitions Department (301) 459-3366

Unit A, Whitacre Mews, 26-34 Stannary Street,
London SE11 4AB, United Kingdom

Library of Congress Control Number: 2015947882
ISBN: 978-0-7618-6660-2 (pbk : alk. paper)

Cover photo Cover photo © Peter Allen. John Ross in Mexico City, 2007.

"The Colonel," from *The Country Between Us* by Carolyn Forché, Copyright © 1981 by Carolyn Forché. Originally appeared in Women's International Resource Exchange. Used by Permission of HarperCollins Publishers.

For Dante and Carla,
and dedicated to the staff of the Hotel Isabel

Contents

Editors' Preface

The only in-person encounter I had with John Ross was listening to him give the lectures you are about to read. His words, without a doubt, changed my life. He sat in front of a class full of journalism students wearing his Mexican garb and looking unlike any reporter I had ever seen, with his cane, drooping eye, and sparsely toothed smile. He proceeded to tell everyone in the room that journalism schools and their creed of "objectivity" were a joke. I learned more during the two lectures I saw him give than I did in all of the journalism classes I have ever taken.

He taught me the importance of "*Ir al lugar de los hechos*. Go to the place where it happened" and showed me the many flaws in journalism today. He gave me a glimpse into a world I didn't know existed, one where it is a moral obligation to be the voice of the people and not the corporations. Ross scoffed at the idea of objectivity, saying that it "distorts the reality," and in a fatherly tone told us, "Folks, there are good things and bad things in this world and we need to take a side."

In a here-and-now society it is easy to get caught up in what is, instead of what could be. Corporate rule, budget cuts, and misinformation from talking heads have robbed my generation of the knowledge we need to better our society and ourselves. While mainstream news is reduced to an entertainment-based reality show, millions of people all over the world are suffering the repercussions of an economic meltdown without any real way to understand why. Instead, what we get is a baseless left-wing versus right-wing debate that makes us turn against our neighbor instead of banding together.

Ross made me ask why, and gave me a thirst for knowledge that no other person has ever given me. After his lectures I bought all three of his books that he had with him and began the process of gaining the valuable "context" that I had failed to learn in my classes.

It has been an honor working on this book. Ross was the most valuable teacher I ever had. I only wish I could have told him the impact he had on my life before he passed away. I hope that this book will do for other aspiring journalists what John Ross, the "investigative poet," did for me.

—Cristalyne Bell, San Isidro, Heredia, Costa Rica, January 2012

I first came to know the work of John Ross in 1987 or '88 while reporting on the Mexican presidential elections/fraud. Ross was already well established as a chronicler of life in what he later called "*El Monstruo*" in his magnum opus on Mexico City. We would not meet in person until 1991, when I visited the D.F. while returning from another trip. We ate supper together in a Chinese restaurant, from which I got horribly ill.

Over the years, our friendship grew. I would visit whenever I was in Mexico, and I would host John's visits to Madison on a string of book tours. John Ross jokingly referred to himself on those trips as a "modern-day Willie Loman," carrying suitcases brimful with newly printed volumes of political writings and poetry. During these visits, I would set up talks at Madison's three main academic institutions (University of Wisconsin, Edgewood College & MATC—now called Madison College), as well as the local progressive bookshop (Rainbow Bookstore Cooperative) and of course on WORT-FM Community Radio.

On one visit, John Ross was in the WORT studios while another host was interviewing John Sayles on air about his recent film, *Men With Guns*. Ross grabbed a phone and called in to the show to critique Sayles on his deal with the Mexican government to allow for filming in the highly militarized Chiapas region. Another visit allowed me to pair up John Ross the poet with comic-folksinger Dave Lippman, a veteran of the solidarity movements with Central America and the Palestinian people.

Occasionally I sent John things—a part for his dilapidated Mac laptop and a "Mao's Pad" (you can guess the text it contained). Visits to Mexico City always brought a depth of insight into local politics and movements that few others could share. On one trip, in 1994, John shared a wealth of details about an armored car robbery that had just taken place that morning, including the personal history of the military officer who had been shot dead during the heist. "It's all about the context," Ross said. "I can't move anywhere else and throw away all those years of context."

In 2004, I was able to credential Ross as my "assistant" to cover the Republican National Convention in New York. As we sat in what should have been a Republicans-only section of seats in Madison Square Garden, Ross joined the cheering crowds as Bush took the stage: "Four More Wars," he shouted. "John," I cautioned, "they're gonna throw us out!" But the nearby secret service agent (complete with earpiece and mini camera) was much more interested in studying the real "taxi-driver" type who sat a few rows down from us (I doubt he made it out of the crowd unquestioned). In 2003, we were together in downtown San Francisco at the outbreak of the invasion of Iraq, and on his last visit to Madison in 2010, I was able to bring him along in the Madison march on that war's anniversary.

John's article on Brad Will was written in part at my kitchen table, and his visit to Waldheim Cemetery (background research for *Murdered by Capitalism*) was scheduled on my phone. But the one thing John Ross ever asked of me, I was unable to do until now. He had collected the best of his lectures to college journalism students into one volume. He wanted to publish these lectures as a counterpoint to a lot of what is taught to aspiring journalists in these schools.

Today, that book is in your hands.

—Norman Stockwell, Madison, WI, Fall 2011

ACKNOWLEDGMENTS

It takes a village. Thank you to everyone who has helped make this book possible, including (but not limited to): Melanie Herzog for her constant support; David Giffey for his lifelong commitment to photography, journalism, art and activism; Larry Hansen and Geoff Bradshaw of Madison College for hosting several of John's lectures; all the staff and volunteers of WORT-FM Community Radio; Lester Doré and Sally Hanner for the wonderful artwork and great food; Catherine Komp and Laura Brickman for their essential contributions; Bob McChesney for his steadfast commitment to a free press; Elizabeth Bell for her invaluable guidance; Denis Moynihan for his support; and Amy Goodman, for being Amy Goodman.

John Ross ¡Presente!

Foreword

There is a general consensus about what the constituent parts of a democratic journalism are:

1. It must provide a rigorous account of people who are in power and people who wish to be in power, in the government, corporate, and nonprofit sectors.
2. It must regard the information needs of all people as legitimate. If anything, the emphasis must be given to the information needs of those without wealth and property. Those with wealth and property always have the information they need to control a society; it is those without such means for whom such information is a necessity.
3. It must have a plausible method to separate truth from lies, or at least to prevent liars from being unaccountable and leading nations into catastrophes—particularly wars, economic crises, and communal discord.
4. It must produce a wide range of informed opinions on the most important issues of our times—not only the transitory concerns of the moment, but also challenges that loom on the horizon. These issues cannot be determined primarily by what people in power are talking about. Journalism must provide the nation's early warning system, so problems can be anticipated, studied, debated, and addressed before they grow to crisis proportions.

This understanding of journalism grows directly from the nation's founders. As Thomas Jefferson wrote: "The way to prevent these irregular interpositions of the people is to give them full information of their affairs thro' the channel of the public papers, and to contrive that those papers should penetrate the whole mass of the people. *The basis of our governments being the opinion of the people*, the very first object should be to keep that right; and were it left to me to decide whether we should have a government without newspapers, or newspapers without a government, I should not hesitate a moment to prefer the latter. *But I should mean that every man should receive those papers and be capable of reading them.*"[1] James Madison famously observed in 1822, "A popular government without popular information or the means of acquiring it, is but a Prologue to a Farce or a Tragedy or perhaps both. Knowledge will forever govern ignorance, and a people who mean to be their own Governors, must arm themselves with the power knowledge gives."[2]

Mainstream journalism in the United States today is light-years away from achieving these criteria, and sometimes appears to be their polar opposite. To some extent, the crisis is inherent in a system of private capitalist control over news media, combined with advertising providing the majority of revenues. As these news media markets invariably tended toward becoming concentrated and noncompetitive, it afforded the owners tremendous political power and tended to marginalize the voices and interests of the poor and working-class. By the first two decades of the 20th century this became a major crisis for American journalism. The solution to the problem was the emergence of professional journalism. This embodied the revolutionary idea that the owner and the editor could be separated, and that the political views of the owner (and advertisers) would not be reflected in the nature of the journalism, except on the editorial page. This was a 180-degree shift from the entire history of American journalism, which was founded on the notion of an explicitly partisan and highly competitive press that played an integral role in the political process. This partisan press remained intact through the 19th century, only to be undermined by the increasing concentration and profitability of the news media.

Under professionalism, news would be determined and produced by trained professionals, and the news would be objective, nonpartisan, factually accurate, and unbiased. Whether there were ten newspapers in a community or only one or two would be mostly irrelevant, because trained journalists—like mathematicians addressing an algebra problem—would all come up with the same news reports. There were no schools of journalism in the United States (or the world, for that matter) in 1900. By the 1920s all the major journalism schools had been established, and by 1923 the American Society of Newspaper Editors was formed and had established a professional code for editors and reporters to follow.

It is important to understand that there is nothing inevitable or "natural" about the type of professional journalism that emerged in the United States in the last century. The professional news values that came to dominate in this country were contested; the journalists' union, the Newspaper Guild, in the 1930s unsuccessfully attempted to have a nonpartisan journalism that was far more critical of all people in power, and viewed itself as the agent of people outside of power to "afflict the comfortable and comfort the afflicted," as Dunne's saying goes. It regarded journalism as a third force independent of both government and big business, and wanted to prohibit publishers from having any control over the content of the news. As the leading history of the formation of the Guild reports: "The idea that the Guild could rebalance the power struggle between public and publisher through a new kind of steward-ship of freedom of the press became a core tenet of their mission as an organization."[3]

This remains a compelling vision of journalism, worthy of being a portion of a good news system, and is still practiced today by some of our best journalists. It is the journalism of I.F. Stone, of Glenn Greenwald, of Bill Moyers, of Amy Goodman, of Naomi Klein, of Jeremy Scahill, and of John Ross.

This practice of journalism was anathema to most publishers, who wanted no part of aggressive reporting on their fellow business owners or the politi-cians they routinely worked with and relied upon for their businesses to be successful. They also were never going to sign away their direct control over the newsroom; editors and reporters had their autonomy strictly at the own-er's discretion. The resulting professionalism was to the owners' liking, for the most part, and more conducive to their commercial and political needs.

The core problem with professional journalism as it crystallized was that it relied far too heavily upon official sources (i.e., people in power) as the appro-priate agenda setters for news and as the "deciders" with regard to the range of legitimate debate in our political culture. There is considerable irony in this development; Walter Lippmann, generally regarded as the leading advocate of professionalism, argued that the main justification for and requirement of profes-sionalism in journalism was that it provide a trained group of independent non-partisan reporters who could successfully and rigorously debunk government (and, implicitly, corporate) spin, not regurgitate it.[4]

This reliance upon official sources—people in power—as setting the le-gitimate agenda and range of debate removed some of the controversy from the news, and it made the news less expensive to produce. It didn't cost much to put reporters where people in political power congregate and report on what they say—certainly a lot less than it cost to send those same reporters around the world on a mission to determine whether the officials in Washing-ton were telling the truth. This gave the news an "establishment" tone. It made reporters careful about antagonizing those in power, upon whom they depended for "access" to their stories.[5] Chris Hedges, the Pulitzer Prize-winning former *New York Times* reporter, describes the reliance on official sources this way: "It is a dirty quid pro quo. The media get access to the elite as long as the media faithfully report what the elite wants reported. The moment that quid pro quo breaks down, reporters—real reporters—are cast into the wilderness and denied access."[6] And it meant that people outside of power had less influence, or that their influence was determined to a certain extent by how people in power regarded them.[7]

This fundamental limitation of professional journalism does not manifest itself in the coverage of those issues where there is rich and pronounced debate between or within leading elements of the dominant political parties. Then journalists have a good deal of room to maneuver, and professional standards can work to assure factual accuracy, balance, and credibility. There tend to be slightly fewer problems in robust political eras, like the 1960s, when mass political movements demand the attention and respect of the powerful.

The real problem with professional journalism becomes evident when political elites do not debate an issue, and march in virtual lockstep. In such a case, professional journalism is, at best, ineffectual and, at worst, pure propaganda. This has often been the case in U.S. foreign policy, where both parties are beholden to an enormous global military complex, and accept the right of the United States, and the United States alone, to invade countries when it suits U.S. interests.[8] In matters of war and foreign policy, journalists who question the basic assumptions and policy objectives, and who attempt to raise issues no one in the leadership of either party wishes to debate, are considered "ideological" and "unprofessional." This has a powerful disciplinary effect upon journalists.[9] The same is true of the capitalist nature of the economy; as Ben Bagdikian has observed, corporate power is as exempt from journalistic scrutiny in the U.S. news media as communism was in the heyday of *Pravda* and *Izvestia*.

Into this maelstrom comes the anti-career and oeuvre of John Ross, a self-described rebel reporter and arch-enemy of J-School journalism. For decades John Ross practiced Jefferson journalism, covering revolutions, rebellions, and reality with the acuity of Tom Paine, the honesty of Albert Camus, the wit of George Carlin, and the prose of Jack Kerouac. In a sane world he would be a household name, and like Tom Paine his words would have moved a nation to greatness. Fortunately, his time may well come, because he has left us these extraordinary lectures on journalism and reporting, words of wisdom for the next generations.

Throughout 2011, as uprisings swept the United States from Madison and Ohio to Wall Street and then everywhere, the chant that animated the legions of protesters was "This Is What Democracy Looks Like."

As you read this extraordinary book, your mind will buzz with the knowledge that "This Is What Journalism Looks Like."

Dr. Robert W. McChesney
Professor of Communication
Center for Global Studies, University of Illinois at Urbana

Introduction

John Ross was a journalist and poet who spent much of his life traveling between the San Francisco Bay area and Mexico. He adopted Mexico City as his home, and wrote and reported from there for both Mexican and U.S. outlets, including *The Nation* and *The Progressive* magazines. With his signature beret and impish grin, Ross practiced "rebel journalism," his reporting style so passionately and colorfully articulated in the lectures collected in this volume.

As these words are written, the disappearance and suspected massacre of 43 students in the state of Guerrero continues to rock Mexico to the core. The horror has mobilized millions of Mexicans who are demanding justice and an end to impunity. It crystallizes, for a global audience, the systemic crisis in Mexico, as the socioeconomic experiment promoted under the banner of NAFTA, the North American Free Trade Agreement, enters its third decade.

One cannot understand the situation in Mexico without context. Like Diego Rivera's epic murals, John Ross crafted stories in the vernacular, writing across formats, from nonfiction "gonzo" journalism, to fiction, to poetry, depicting Mexico in the thrall of U.S.-imposed, post-Cold War neo-liberalism. "Our words should be well chosen," Ross writes in Lecture Four. "Not just strung together from left to right but considered both for their accuracy and their music. Our words should be ready to paint the picture."

He once told an editor at the now-shuttered *San Francisco Bay Guardian*, "You have to go where the story is." John Ross did just that, walking amidst the rubble of Mexico City after the 1985 earthquake, reporting for the Pacific News Service. On the day that NAFTA took effect, January 1, 1994, thousands of indigenous people rebelled in Mexico's southernmost state, Chiapas, calling themselves "Zapatistas." Ross was not far from the action. While reporters for corporate news outlets sped around Chiapas chasing the elusive Zapatistas without success, John Ross, who had lived among Mexico's indigenous people, traveled on foot into the highlands. He went to the source of the story, and interviewed key participants in the historic uprising. Ross's reporting led to his book on the Zapatista uprising, *Rebellion from the Roots*, a must-read for anyone seeking to understand what happened there.

Shortly after the uprising, I also went down to San Cristóbal de las Casas, the capital city of Chiapas, reporting for Pacifica Radio's WBAI. Like Ross, I avoided the expensive hotels that were filling up with Western reporters. Late at night, in the accommodations I found on the edge of the city, I was contacted and told to rush to a clandestine press conference. The rebels felt it would have been far too dangerous for them to send word to the hotels in the center of town, where the reporters from the corporate news companies were holed up. Subcomandante Marcos, the Zapatista leader, said he wanted in his first press conference to address Mexican radio stations. Radio, he explained, is the form of communication closest to the people. The Zapatista leadership was there to explain their uprising and to answer our questions. Later, enraged that I was the only U.S.-based journalist to have recorded Marcos and the others, one of the reporters from a major network tried (and failed) to steal my tape, which I was sharing anyway. I can imagine what John Ross would have said.

Rodolfo Acuña, historian at California State University at Northridge, is considered one of the founders of Chicano studies. He wrote recently, "In less than twenty years, Mexico has been taken over by the drug cartels, the *ejidos* [communal farmlands] have legally been made vulnerable, Mexico has twelve more billionaires, and the Mexican government is complicit with the cartels in incinerating the 43 Normalistas [the missing students in Guerrero]. On top of all that the Mexican Constitution of 1917 has been thrown in a garbage dump… In the span of fifteen years, the neoliberal takeover has seen the privatization of higher education, the Congress, and the Supreme Court." This is the ravaging of a society by unbridled corporate power and corruption that John Ross captured so brilliantly with his words.

From the Zapatista uprising to the war in Iraq to the movement against Wal-Mart, from Oaxaca and the murder of journalist Brad Will to the history of union organizer Joe Hill over a century ago, John Ross covered it all, with passion, with a fierce commitment to justice, and in solidarity with the underdog. He is no longer here in person to inspire us, but his words remain—the wry, unyielding words of a true rebel journalist.

Read on, and take his lessons to heart.

Amy Goodman
Host and executive producer
Democracy Now!/democracynow.org

Part I

Handing It Down:
Four Lectures on Rebel Journalism

"A bad person cannot be a good journalist."   —Ryszard Kapuściński [1]

ABOUT THE LECTURES

These lectures were first delivered to a classroom of students at San Francisco's New College in the Fall of 2006. It was here that Ross developed the concept for a series of talks that he later took on tour around the United States, delivering them in various forms to students at universities and community colleges. In March 2010 he delivered two of these at Madison College. Independent journalist Brad Will was killed in Oaxaca, México, during the time that Ross first delivered these lectures. The lectures have been edited only slightly for publication, and sometimes refer to events and places that were surrounding Ross as he first delivered them in San Francisco's Mission District.

Lecture One

What Are We Doing Here?

I.

I'll let you answer the question of what we are doing here later. I have another question first: Who is Josh Wolf? You don't have to raise your hands. Josh Wolf is what used to be called in the Cosa Nostra a stand-up guy. Josh Wolf is sitting in the federal can over there across the bay in a burg called Pleasanton, which can't be all that pleasant, because he refuses to turn over videotape he shot of an anti-capitalist march that got out of hand on Mission Street in July 2004. Josh Wolf has now been locked down for over 70 days and he will sit there for the entire life of the Grand Jury because the court has refused to hear any further appeals. By resisting such coercion, Josh Wolf is practicing rebel journalism. Josh Wolf! Live like him!

OK class, this seminar is called "rebel journalism" just in case you wandered into the wrong room. What is "rebel journalism" anyway? Just some catchy scam to sucker in young and not so young media studies grad students at eccentric, overpriced institutes of higher learning?

Is rebel journalism "journalism about rebellion"? You bet your booty. That's the content of rebel journalism. Rebel journalism advocates rebellion; in fact good rebel journalism incites rebellion.

So who is a rebel journalist? Well, hang on, I don't know about this "journalist" stuff. It sounds snooty. I call myself a reporter; it's a lot closer to the street.

But is a rebel reporter just one who covers rebellion? That seems to depend upon which side of the barricade you wind up on. A lot of hotshot corporate reporters—Rob Collier, the *San Francisco Chronicle*'s foreign editor is one—covered the Contra rebellion in Nicaragua from the side of the Contras.

A good rebel reporter doesn't just take notes on rebellion. A good rebel reporter incites rebellion, makes people angry, encourages organization, offers them hope that another world is possible. A rebel reporter is a participant in rebellion or resistance or revolution or whatever you want to call the struggle for social change. Like the Zapatistas, our words are our weapons.

So who are some rebel reporters? I spoke about Josh Wolf. By the time he's out, Josh will have served more time in prison than any other U.S. reporter who has ever gone to jail for refusing to turn over his or her sources.[1] The previous record—168 days—is held by a Houston-based reporter who refused to reveal her sources on a murder story.

Judith Miller, who ran 11 mendacious front-page stories in the *New York Times* "documenting" Saddam Hussein's fictitious Weapons of Mass Destruction and provided public justification for the massacre of hundreds of thousands of Iraqis, only did 85 days, and not for war crimes either. It was because she balked at finking out a neo-con pal who had outed Joe Wilson's wife as a CIA operative.[2]

You ask what's wrong with outing a CIA operative? Nothing. It's an act of rebel reporting, in fact. The only ethical act Judith Miller ever perpetrated.

Anyway, Josh has a lot of time on his hands these days and jail is not such a bad place to report from. I did my first English-language story from Terminal Island Federal Penitentiary doing a year on a draft beef back in 1964. "What To Do in Jail" it was titled, a kind of primer for imprisoned activists.

Someone who had been in jail at the School of Americas protests in Fort Benning for a couple of months told me recently, "Jail is like visiting a poor country." Almost everyone there is poor and has a story to tell. When rebel reporters go to jail, they should consider themselves foreign correspondents.

What burns me up about Josh Wolf is that reporters refuse to accept him as a real reporter. To these J-School "Richie Riches," Josh is some post-adolescent anarchist punk blogger, anything but a member of their elite profession. We will talk about J-School at length down the pike.

Josh Wolf is part of a long-running continuum of rebel reporting in America, reporters that most often got dissed by the J-School illuminati. John Reed was a rebel reporter almost a hundred years ago. He was a talented labor organizer from Portland who promoted the 1915 Patterson silk strike into national prominence and stood on the podium shoulder to shoulder with Big Bill Haywood and "the Rebel Girl"—Elizabeth Gurley Flynn. Reed rode into Mexico with Pancho Villa in 1913 at the height of that first great revolution of landless farmers, and his book *Insurgent Mexico* still stands up as some of the best reportage from that landmark uprising. He was a founder of the U.S. Communist Party, but worked for the capitalist press, and his witness in revolutionary Russia, only a part of which is recorded in his masterwork, *Ten*

Days That Shook the World, is legendary. Warren Beatty played him in the movies.

John Reed died young and on the job, of typhoid fever in Estonia, covering the civil war that engulfed the Soviet Union right after the revolution. His bones are still buried in the Kremlin wall.

John Reed! Live like him!

La Jornada, the left paper in Mexico City, once erred in labeling me "the new John Reed covering a New Mexican revolution," referring to my work on the Zapatista rebellion. I can assure you the resemblance is merely phonetic.

The first rebel reporter I came to know was a guy named I.F. Stone.[3] This was really an accident of birth. My parents, both of whom were Broadway commies, spent summers at Fire Island where Izzy and Esther summered too—as did the Boudins. Leonard Boudin, a radical attorney whose daughter became an infamous "Weatherwoman," was Paul Robeson's lawyer. All of them were in or out of the Communist Party and had known each other for decades. My mom had gone to summer camp with Leonard's wife Jean and I sometimes babysat Kathy, who did almost 30 years in jail for a bank holdup—it was probably all my fault.

I would often see Izzy out there on the sun porch, scribbling and ripping up newspapers like a madman, and wondered what he did for a living. I.F. Stone was stone deaf and never turned on his hearing aid. He didn't like to be disturbed when he was working, his youngest son Chris warned me.

My mom finally cleared up the mystery of what Izzy was doing out there on the porch. She showed me his classic exposé of the 1952 CIA-sponsored overthrow of the Árbenz government in Guatemala—the democratically elected president had threatened expropriation of United Fruit properties. I got it. Izzy was an investigative reporter.

By then, I.F. Stone was publishing his own weekly insider newsletter—the HUAC witch-hunters coveted the subscription list—but he had worked as a beat reporter for the *New York Post* when it was still a left paper, and for *PM* newspaper which refused all advertising, and the *New York Compass*, a U.S. Communist Party front that had the best horse-racing handicappers in town. And this at a time when New York City had seven daily newspapers—my pop wrote the "So This Is Broadway" column for the *World Telegram and Sun*. Enough nostalgia.

I.F. Stone was a sharp stone in the Eisenhower administration's shoe. What he looked for in every story—he read them from the bottom up before literally ripping the page apart—was what was missing. What was not in the story? And that's the part he wrote about. Without him, as Bertolt Brecht writes in "To Posterity," the rulers would have been more secure.

I.F. Stone! Live like him!

Finally I want to give you a role model who isn't usually found in the rebel reporter repertory. His real name was Joseph Hillström, but history calls him Joe Hill and he was a trouble-making troubadour. Joe was a founding member of the Industrial Workers of the World, the Wobblies. He held one of the first red cards and organized the stevedores up and down the West Coast, traveling from town to town singing subversive lyrics to popular songs and spreading the news. Singers, songwriters, pickers, poets have always been rebel reporters, bringing the news to the public plazas.

> Joe Hill is my name and
> songwriting gained me fame
> The copper bosses gunned me down
> In 1915 in a Mormon town
> But my only real crime
> Was dreaming up rhymes
> For the working class of people.
> It's doggerel, the bosses critiqued.
> We gonna have to put this dog to sleep,
> But what they forgot to exorcise
> Went on to organize.
> Went on to organize.
> I sang for my supper
> and I sang for my bread
> but singing for the coppers,
> I'd be better off dead.
> I'm a radical rapper
> And I ain't gonna chill
> Until my fellow workers
> Have eaten their fill

That's part of my Joe Hill rap from *Murdered By Capitalism: 150 Years of Life & Death on the American Left*. Well, I thought it was a rap but my son, the king of rap, says it's some kind of Woody Guthrie sh*t.

In Mexican culture, the "*corrido*" or ballad is sort of a musical newspaper. Back in 1974, my pal Salomé Gutiérrez who runs the Del Bravo Recording Studio, Record Store and Greyhound bus station down to the border at Del Rio, Texas, had a group in the studio out in west "San Atone" when a neighbor rushed in to tell him about the escape of the notorious drug dealer Fred Carrasco from the federal courthouse downtown. Two were killed. Salomé sat down and wrote a *corrido* and cut it right away with the band. Then he took the cart over to a local station that played *corridos* from dawn to dusk and it got aired all day—it was the first news many folks in San Antonio had of the big breakout.

So where is all this going? The point is that the *corridos*, the blues, poems, raps, tags, and blogs, all this popular communicating, is a radical way of reporting the news from the bottom up.

II.

Now we come to the part where I emit pearls of useless advice. Useless because you have to live this stuff to know it. You don't have to listen. You won't be quizzed.

The first thing you need to know is that you do not have a career in journalism. Forget about your career. You have an obligation—to tell the story of those who entrust you with theirs, to tell the truth about the way the world works. In Mexico, we call this an *"oficio,"* an office of responsibility to the community. You serve the community. You don't have a career.

In this respect, rebel reporting is the polar opposite of J-School journalism, which is all about personal and corporate power, about conserving the power of the class from whose loins most J-Schoolers spring. J-School pretends that you have a "career" in corporate journalism, that you too can be a big media star like Geraldo Rivera or Christiane Amanpour. J-School teaches you how to lie for a living, how to sell your skills to transnational media consortiums for an ounce of flesh. J-School teaches you how to promote class oppression, consumerism, racism. How to justify genocide and the destruction of the planet. The status quo.

J-Schoolers are not reporters—they are careerists. J-School teaches you how your career is so much more important than speaking truth to power. It teaches you how to watch your words and carefully select your stories so as not to offend the editors and jeopardize your career track. J-School teaches you to adopt cynicism as your moral compass. The news? Who gives a f*ck about the news? The news, as the British press baron Lord Thomson never failed to remind his reporters, is just what fills the blank spaces between the advertisements.

I myself have never passed through the portals of a journalism school except to disabuse the inmates of their goals. I am a freelancer. I am free to carry a lance and tilt at windmills with all the righteousness of the Quixote—only my lance is as long as this [a Pentel Rolling Writer]. I have been a freelancer for nearly 50 years now, a half a century; it's hard for even me to believe it.

Oh sure, I've had my flirtations with the corporate press. I was Mexico correspondent for the *San Francisco Examiner*, then called "the Monarch of the Dailies," indeed the flagship Hearst paper, for a few years and once ran ten straight front-page stories after the election was stolen from Cuauhtémoc Cárdenas in 1988. I came on board soon after Willie Hearst had taken the reins. His uncle Randolph Hearst never recovered from Patty's defection to the Symbionese Liberation Army. It was like a soap opera. Young Will brought in a bunch of dangerous characters—Hunter S. Thompson, Zippy the Pinhead, and me. But the *Examiner* was the corporate press and the fun didn't last very long.

It's true that I'm still on the masthead of the *Bay Guardian*, although I don't know why. Bruce Brugmann has ripped it off a couple of times when I challenged his politics on the pages of his own paper. At the *Bay Guardian*, the news hole fills the space between boutique ads. The *Bay Guardian* is the corporate press with a little less tolerance for Savage Capitalism.

But by and large, for the past 50 years I've been a freelancer. I am beholden to no one, corporate entity or otherwise. I don't work alongside the corporate press. I run away from the pack. I am free to select my own stories and how to frame them, my own skew. I am free to choose what words to use and I am also free to sleep under bridges and lose all my teeth. I live in a hotel room in the old quarter of Mexico City that is as threadbare as my wardrobe. I had no health care until I got to be an old man, and the government I have been trying to overthrow all my life declared me eligible to receive a small monthly stipend because I had worked enough hours in my life trying to organize the working class to rise up against the bosses.

But even if I'll never have any disposable income, I can't complain. I call my own shots. I agree with what John Leonard wrote of me (in *Harper's* magazine): "Ross is in no more danger of selling out than he is of finding a buyer." That's who I am.

So this is my advice: avoid J-School like a poison.

Rebel reporters practice investigative reporting. They investigate who is getting screwed, who is doing the screwing, and how those who are getting screwed can reverse this equation. Rebel reporters are always finding flashlights, finding flashlights as Ed Sanders describes in his remarkable City Lights volume *Investigative Poetry*. Flashlights to peer into the darkness. It is our *oficio*.

Rebel reporters practice advocacy journalism—that is, we stand for something. J-School teaches you the opposite. Rebel reporters practice participatory journalism. They not only stand behind their stories but stand inside them. Rebel reporters become their stories.

For the J-Schoolers, the highest ethical principle is so-called objectivity. Rebel reporters say that "objectivity" is an instrument of class oppression that gives greater voice to the oppressor than the oppressed. Rebel reporters don't arrive at the gates of Dachau[4] in a taxi and ask to interview the Commandant just to get his side of the story. Sure, rebel reporters need to know what the oppressor is saying, to dissect it and rip it apart, but we don't really have all that much time to listen to their lies.

III.

The Midnight Special
Burrows into the bowels
Of the North American nightmare
Like a sleek silver tapeworm
Consuming the body fat of
The most over-stuffed nation
In the known universe.
The rules for travel
Are posted at the terminals:
Do not leave luggage unattended.
Report all suspicious activity.
Protect your back at all times
From homegrown suicide bombers,
Homeland Security, GMO corn,
AIDS, the Anti-Christ,
The New York Times.
I scratch out a map
In a wilderness of white paper
That bloodies the nation
With crimson headlines
From sea to stinking sea.
I can no longer parse the horror.
The scales have fallen
From my snake eyes:
There is no lie worth dying for.
Ir al lugar de los hechos.
Go to the place where it happens.
That is the first rule of the finding.
They will not want you there
But you will learn much
From their fury.
Write it all down
Right away in your head.
Do not let the details leak out
No matter how badly they beat you,
Do not forget their faces.
Do not forget their eyes.
Do not believe everything
They say. Do not believe
Anything you read.

That's a poem from a my chapbook *Bomba!* I read it to the J-Schoolers when they invite me to yap at them.

Back home in Mexico City, my "*gremio*," or labor group, is the *Hermandad de Periodistas Rebeldes*. We have two members and two by-laws. The first is "*ir al lugar de los hechos*." Go to where it happened. Desk stories just don't live. You just can't sit there at your console, punching it all up. Googling doesn't get you there. You never see who it is you are talking to on e-mail or the cell phone. Rebel reporters do not practice virtual journalism.

Rebel reporters, like Kerouac and Cassady, are on the road. *Ir al lugar de los hechos.* When you have been there, the story will become part of you. You will taste it, feel it, hear it, smell it. I have walked in muddy fields hunting day-old corpses. The smell never leaves you. Once I covered a huge fireworks explosion at a candy market not far from my home in Mexico City. Sixty people had been blown apart on the eve of the fiesta of the Virgin of Guadalupe. Shards of their flesh were everywhere, glazed with the melted candy. The stench of caramelized human flesh always comes to me when I pass La Merced now. It is imprinted in my olfactory memory.

Go to the place where it happens. Remember, getting to the story is half the story, so travel slow. The best stories are way far away from power so it will take you a while to get there. Use the time wisely. Others are going there too and will tell you why. Study the landscape.

Here is how I got to one of the enormous rallies that the leftist Andrés Manuel López Obrador called after the 2006 Mexican presidential election was stolen from him:

> On the Saturday before the march, I walked the highway down from Morelos state with a calloused handful of campesinos who tilled plots on the *ejido* of Anenecuilco, Emiliano Zapata's home turf, the land for which this incorrupt-ible revolutionary was martyred. "We have an obligation to fix this fraud—the General would not forgive us if we did not try," a weather-beaten farmer named Saúl Franco avowed. "If Zapata was alive, he would be with us today," Saúl suggested, echoing the hand-written sign he had slung around his neck.[5]

Often you will not be received well when you get to the place where it happens. You will be seen as an interloper, a bothersome witness. I've been run out of towns, thrown out of whole countries and hauled off to the pokey for poking my proboscis into conflictive situations that did not allegedly concern me. In such situations, I always invoke those lines of the great Salvadoran revolutionary poet Roque Dalton: "and my veins do not end in me/but in the unanimous blood / of all those who struggle / for love / for life / for the things. . ."[6]

Here's a lesson I learned by going to the place where it happens. An unlicensed community radio station run by the Huave community on the sandbars south of Juchitán, Oaxaca, had been threatened with mayhem by the military. I hiked into San Francisco del Mar to talk with the folks who ran Radio Huave. I don't really do interviews anymore. I just go and talk with the principals. But no one around the station wanted to talk to me. In fact, they called the local gendarmes who drove up in a pick-up, about ten of them, armed with clubs and long guns. First thing, the Comandante grabs my notebook and starts ripping out pages. I complain that these are notes to other stories and he hands back the crumpled pages—and then rips out other pages from the notebook. Then he confiscates my mini-recorder and escorts me to the collective taxi and tells me never to come back to Huave country.

When I run this egregious violation of freedom of expression to Ramón Vera, who edits *Ojarasca*, the indigenous supplement of *La Jornada* to which I sometimes contribute, he observes that the Huaves probably took me for a government spy and the police were only protecting their community radio station. You learn stuff like this when you *ir al lugar de los hechos*.

Now that I'm on a roll, here is another cautionary tale from the cave of my memories. Once in Cochabamba, Bolivia, I was allowed to enter into a police station where prisoners from the Chapare, farmers who grew coca, were being tortured. You could hear their cries out in the street—and it was a residential street so everyone who lived there knew. After a while, I was ushered into the Capitán's office. The room was large and very dark, the blinds had been drawn and his desk lamp blinded me. It was one of those "we-have-ways-of-making-you-talk" scenes.

You could hear the thumps and the groans on the other side of the wall. I sat down and handed the Capitán my business card, which in those days read "John Ross, poeta/periodista" (poet/journalist.) There was a painful silence. The groans continued. Finally, he leaned forward to ask me who my favorite poet was. We sat there and talked poetry for a while and then I went home and wrote a story about the poetry-loving torturer. You can't get one of these stories on Google.

The second by-law of the *Hermandad de Periodistas Rebeldes* is simple: *palabras hasta hechos*. Words into deeds. Here the guiding principle is that you can't write anything you don't believe. And your *oficio* obligates you to act upon your beliefs. To be congruent with your words.

Getting the story is not the whole story. Acting upon it, bringing it home, comes next. Back in 1987, I had been working in Latin America for a few years, doing a lot of stories on how the crushing foreign debt was starving out *los de abajo* (those down below). Corrupt governments were paying out obscene debt services to transnational banks just to wheedle more cash while people were going hungry and infant mortality rates were zooming. So, being unemployed, I decided to go north to where the story happened, the belly of the beast, and declare myself on hunger strike on the doorsteps of the murderers—Wall Street, the Bank of America, the International Monetary Fund and World Bank, which are right across the street from each other a few blocks from the White House. The goal was to starve myself to death and transform my words into deeds.

I dressed up in a three-piece pinstripe suit I had once bought to interview Alan García, the first time he was president of Peru. I never got the interview, but I still had the suit. I smeared it with fake blood and stuffed fake money

into the pockets and painted up my face like a Mexican death mask. The
Death Banker Hunger Strike lasted 26 days and it was nearly the death of me.
But it did make my point. We just can't write about injustice. We have the
oficio of turning our words into deeds.

That's it for this first session. I'm going to get out of here with that Roque
Dalton poem I quoted before. Jack Hirschman, our poet laureate, is probably
the most luminous translator of Roque's words but here's my version:

LIKE YOU[7]

I, like you,
Love love,
Life,
The sweet enchantment
Of things,
The blue countryside
In the days of January

My blood also leaps
And my eyes leak laughter
That has known
Its flood of tears,
I believe the world is beautiful,
That poetry is the bread
Of everyone.

And that my veins
Do not end in me
But in the unanimous blood
Of those who struggle
For life,
Love,
The things,
The countryside and the bread,
The poetry of everyone.

OK class, your homework assignment is to take these words to heart and
also to answer the question with which we began today. "What are we doing
here anyway?"

Lecture Two

The Global Beat:
Covering Global Resistance to Globalization

I.

Cuando muere una lengua
las cosas divinas,
estrellas, sol y luna;
las cosas humanas,
pensar y sentir,
no se reflejan ya
en ese espejo.

Cuando muere una lengua,
todo lo que hay en el mundo,
mares y ríos,
animales y plantas,
ni se piensan, ni pronuncian
con atisbos y sonidos,
que no existen ya.

Cuando muere una lengua,
entonces se cierra
a todos los pueblos del mundo
una ventana, una puerta,
un asomarse
de modo distinto
a cuanto es ser y vida en la tierra.

Cuando muere una lengua,
sus palabras de amor,
entonación de dolor y querencia.
tal vez viejos cantos,
relatos, discursos, plegarias,
nadie, cual fueron,
alcanzará a repetir.

Cuando muere una lengua,
ya muchas han muerto
y muchas pueden morir.
Espejos para siempre quebrados,
sombra de voces
Para siempre acalladas:
la humanidad se emprobrece.

Bueno, this is a poem translated from the Aztec by the master translator of Aztec poetry Miguel León Portilla.[1] This is what it says in English:

When a language dies,
The divine things,
Stars, sun and moon,
The human things,
To think and to feel,
No longer are reflected
In this mirror.

When a language dies,
All that there is in this world,
Seas and rivers,
Animals and plants,
Are not thought, do not say
With hints and sounds,
That they do not exist now.

When a language dies,
A window and a door
Are closed up to all the world's people.
No more will they be shown
A different view
Of what it means to be, and life on earth.

When a language dies,
Its words of love,
Intonations of pain and caring,
Perhaps the old songs,
The old stories, speeches, the prayers,
No one no matter who

Will be able to repeat them again.

When a language dies,
Many have died now
And many more will die soon,
Mirrors forever broken,
Shadows of voices
Forever silenced.
Humanity grows poorer.

This may seem an oblique way to open a session I call "The Global Beat: Covering Global Resistance to Globalization," but this incantation is all about demon globalization and how it attacks and impacts humanity. Globalization diminishes us. "Humanity grows poorer."

Globalization homogenizes us into one faceless mass of consumers, slaves to the market. Globalization obliterates diversity. The globalizers would have everyone speaking in English, the lowest-common-denominator consumer language. Globalization kills languages and the peoples who speak them. You can count on two hands the last speakers of Cucapá, Kumiai, Paipai, language systems of people who live in the Baja California desert an hour from Tijuana, that most globalized of tourist traps.

Rebel reporters confront and expose the corporate globalization of the planet, the globalization of greed. But rebel reporters also report on the resistance to globalization, the global resistance, from down below. Rebel reporters defy the market and homogenization. Rebel reporters champion singularity and the uniqueness of all things. Rebel reporters live in the present, but defend and honor what came before, the past. Rebel reporters rescue what is being lost. "Everywhere and always, go after that which is lost," counsels the poet Carolyn Forché. This is our job.

What am I saying here? Reference points are probably in order. What do we mean by "resistance"? From the standpoint of social physics, resistance is pushing back against the forces pressing down upon us. Pushing back looks like this: [Holds up back cover of *The War Against Oblivion: Zapatista Chronicles 1994–2000*]. This is a picture of two young Zapatista women— one has a baby wrapped up on her back—putting their hands on a grizzled soldier and pushing him off their land. See the look of disbelief on his mug? His automatic weapon dangling uselessly at his side? This photo—which was taken by a colleague, Pedro Valtierra—is a picture of what resistance looks like. Pushing back.

Resistance seems to follow rejection and refusal. It is more proactive, takes the initiative. Resistance precedes rebellion, rising up, a revolution, the process of creating radical change. Radical, as in "from the roots."

How do we connect to globalization and how does it connect to us? "Globalization" and "global" are not synonymous. "Global" describes commonalities of those who live on the planet. "Globalization" describes the commodification of the planet. Global resistance is the pushing back of those who refuse to submit to the globalization pressing down upon them where they live. "Where will we go after the last border? Where will we fly after the last sky?" cries the Palestinian poet Mahmoud Darwish.

Globalization is capitalism on steroids, with all the mood swings that drug triggers. Globalization is cruel and savage capitalism. Globalization cannot be contained in any one country. Globalization is free to crash through borders and annihilate people who don't speak the right language. Globalization operates without government constraints. In fact, globalization replaces governments and turns them into business agents for transnational capital.

The almighty market is globalization's maximum god; its religion is neoliberal mumbo jumbo. The market is oracle and judge. Globalization is god and Wall Street is its messenger. They lie when they say that the market is amoral, it doesn't take sides. That it doesn't care. What they mean is that it doesn't care about us. The market makes for few winners, few boats rise. The rest of us drown in the flood.

The temples in which the globalizers sing their hosannas are called the International Monetary Fund (IMF), the World Bank, the World Trade Organization (WTO), the World Water Forum, or just about anything that has prefixed the word "world" to their ambition. The World Bank and the IMF operate out of Washington. They preach a doctrine called "structural adjustment." They will only lend money to countries that abide by the dictates of structural adjustment. They are kind of like quack chiropractors. Instead of adjusting, they crush the spines of the people they treat.

Structural adjustment means privatizing, selling off what belongs to the people and is administrated by the state, to the highest transnational bidder— the natural resources, the transportation systems, the telephone company, electricity generation, health care, the labor of the people. The *pueblo* is left naked and unprotected and every morning it costs more to get on the bus. The fate of the people is left to the whims of their cursed market.

Rebel reporters scoff at the omnipotence of the market. Rebel reporters reach behind the curtain, rip the masks off the Masters of the Universe, and demystify the market. Rebel reporters integrate the pain that globalization inflicts upon humanity and go to the place where it happens. Where the forest has been laid waste and the sea poisoned. Where the people rise up in resistance.

The World Trade Organization is the junior partner in this unholy trinity. While the IMF and the World Bank and other international bloodsuckers snort up billions in usurious debt service in exchange for fresh loans to foment the corruption of Latin American governments, draining the content of its capital like Dracula's mamas, the WTO is the commercial juggernaut by which the transnationals of the North invade and conquer the largely impoverished, darkly-complected but resource-rich nations of the South.

The Masters of the Universe have delegated the WTO to rule world trade. It has supra-national powers—that is, its decisions prevail over national laws. For example, if Mexican Indians object to the dumping of transgenic corn by the Cargill Corporation, the world's largest privately held conglomerate, the Cargill Corporation can go to the WTO and punish Mexico for perpetrating a "restraint of trade," which is criminal blasphemy against the "free" market. This is what they are trying to sell us, but we're not buying.

Globalization is hardly global. Globalization is an instrument by which the global North extracts the wealth and natural resources of the global South, annexes their economies through debt service, and forces the Wal-Martization of the world: displacing local providers, local businesses, national industries, and wrecking economies of scale.

This is not some arcane economic theory packed away in the stacks of your university library. This is as close as your neighborhood Safeway or Wal-Mart. This is as close as the Mexican men just outside walking in pairs down San Francisco's Valencia Street, looking for work, any work, in the mornings. The North American Free Trade Agreement (NAFTA), is the beacon of globalization. It has dumped so much bad corn in Mexico that millions have abandoned their plots and headed north. Some made it across the desert and came to San Pancho.

To shop at Wal-Mart.

Wal-Mart is where globalization comes home. Fact: in 2005, Wal-Mart opened a new store somewhere in the world every day of the year, sometimes two. Fact: if Wal-Mart were a country, it would rank among the top 15 nations in the world.[2] Fact: Wal-Mart accounts for 10% of all China's manufactured exports and has entered into a strategical alliance with that tyrannical People's Republic. Wal-Mart is the leader of the pack in the race to the bottom. Wal-Mart is archly anti-union, misogynist, and shamelessly exploits undocumented immigrant labor. Wal-Mart is the perfect place to begin a story on globalization.

Wal-Mart spread south in a hurry, following NAFTA's footprints. It operates over 700 megastores in Mexico.[3] It is the nation's number one employer and dominates retail sales.

I got to know Wal-Mart a few years back when I did a story for the *Progressive Magazine* about a new megastore that had just opened its doors amidst the great ruins of Teotihuacan, the first corn culture in the Americas and probably its first city, on the northern flank of the capital. Although Wal-Mart had taken pains to camouflage it, the store was actually quite visible from the crown of the Pyramid of the Sun out there in the third archaeological perimeter. One construction worker got fired for telling reporters how he kept digging up artifacts in the parking lot—the company ordered him to haul them off to the dump and keep his lips sealed.

Teotihuacan is a sacred site. Wal-Mart has ripped up sacred sites all over the U.S. west to build big box stores. Wal-Mart kills ancient cultures and sacrifices them on the bloody altar of out-of-control consumerism.

Doing the Teotihuacan story was like covering Huntington's "Clash of Civilizations?" The *ambulantes,* or street vendors, and the market people kept sabotaging construction because Wal-Mart was going to put them out of business. Indigenous people came from all over the country and blockaded the archeological zone in protest. A police car was set afire. Indians said putting the Wal-Mart there would be genocide.

Finally the day the store was to open, the government sent a team of archeologists to check once more for buried artifacts. They dug a big hole between the cash registers at the head of aisles five and six and the opening had to be postponed.

The next week the Teotihuacan Wal-Mart was really going to open. There were a few thousand people on line in the parking lot, waiting for the free giveaways, but the store remained locked. The cash registers wouldn't connect to the computers in Bentonville, Arkansas, where every single Wal-Mart sale in the world is registered. This is how globalization works, folks. The riot squad had to be called to keep the mob from storming the store. The gods of Teotihuacan must have been working overtime that day.

Wal-Mart is the poster boy for what the framers of NAFTA call "convergence," that is that the same product will be sold in the same stores at the same price on both sides of the border. NAFTA is the stalking horse of globalization, one of the first free trade agreements or treaties (in Mexico, NAFTA is called a "treaty," in the U.S. it is called an "agreement") ever signed between the South and the North. Whatever you want to call it, it's a crime against the people.

NAFTA was never popular with the American people. No one ever demanded NAFTA except the transnational corporations. Labor, environmentalists, the human rights movement forcefully opposed it and it only cleared the House by 34 out of 435 votes. Clinton heaped up billions in pork to buy those 34 votes. The Mexican people never got to vote on NAFTA either.

In its first 13 years, NAFTA decimated Mexican agriculture, dumping millions of tons of highly subsidized U.S. corn. According to a 2004 Carnegie Endowment study,[4] agricorporations can receive up to $2,100 an acre to grow corn on the other side of the border. And 40% of that is genetically modified to crush out Mexican seed. GMO corn is a trick on Mexico. The dumping of U.S. corn will homogenize 600 distinct families of Mexican corn, the oldest corn on the planet, the first corn, domesticated eight millennia ago in the *altiplano* of what is now the city of Puebla. In Mexico, they say *"no hay país sin maíz"*—there is no country without corn—but if things keep going like they are and the terminator seed takes over, they are going to have to change the name of the country to Monsanto-landia.

The Carnegie Endowment study showed that the massive importation of NAFTA corn has forced about 6,000,000 farmers and their families off the land. They couldn't compete and so they jumped into the immigration stream. Over 5,000[5] Mexicans and Central Americans, many of them displaced *campesinos*, have lost their lives trying to get across the border since NAFTA was inked to take a job that no North American will work.

They drown in the Río Bravo and the All-American Canal, fall into the *barrancas* on La Rumorosa, desiccate out in the desert west of Yuma, are bitten by rattlesnakes scurrying through south Texas, suffocate in boxcars on sidings in Iowa, are crushed dashing across dangerous freeways, and shot down by *la Migra* when they try to get away. Over 5,000! Each one of them is a story about globalization. They are what globalization is all about. There's your story.

II.

Of course, the other side of the globalization of greed story is the globalization of resistance. Take for example this story in *Rebellion From the Roots: Indian Uprising in Chiapas*:

> The pitch-black night suddenly came alive with darting shadows. The slap-slap of rubber boots against the slick pavement echoed throughout the hushed neighborhoods on the periphery of town. Sleepy *chuchos* rose in their patios, stretched and bayed, their howling catching from block to block, barrio to barrio. Across the narrow Puente Blanco, up the rutted Centenario Diagonal, down General Utrilla from the marketplace district, dark columns marched in military cadences. With their features cancelled behind ski-masks and bandannas that left their collective breath hanging in the still mountain air like vapors from a past too many Mexicans do not want to recognize as being very present, the *sin rostros* (those without faces) advanced on the city of San Cristóbal de las Casas, the throne of the Mayan highlands of Chiapas, Mexico's southernmost and arguably its most impoverished and indigenous state, soon after midnight January 1, 1994, in the very first hour of the North American Free Trade Agreement. So it began, the Zapatista rebellion.

The Zapatistas knew that NAFTA would mean the death knell for the Maya, the People of Corn—the *Popul Vuh* and the *Chilam Balam*, the Mayan sacred books, say they are actually made from the corn. Now the inundation of cheap, poison NAFTA corn would prevent the People of the Corn from selling in the domestic market. They would lose their land and no longer be Indians.

I've been privileged to have accompanied the Zapatista rebellion since its earliest hours. In fact, I wrote the first story about the EZLN (*Ejército Zapatista de Liberación Nacional*) months before the rebellion surfaced. In May 1993, there had been a shoot-out between the military and an unknown armed band just outside Ocosingo, the gateway to the Lacandón jungle, and I went to the place where it happened. People told me stuff, I saw some revealing documentation. I wrote the story that July, but no one would publish it. Science fiction, one editor told me. NAFTA was up before congress that summer, and both Mexican president Salinas and U.S. president Bill Clinton wanted to make sure no word of the impending uprising leaked out because it might upset the applecart and be bad for business. Finally, on October 23, 1993, my piece ran in an eccentric northern California weekly, the *Anderson Valley Advertiser*, which scooped the world on the rebellion by six weeks.[6]

The Zapatista story is all about the globalization of resistance. In 1996, the Zapatistas called a conference in the middle of the Lacandón jungle "In Defense of Humanity and Against Neo-Liberalism." The event was called the "Intergaláctica" and people from all five continents (and maybe some from other planets) came and danced in the mud. It was at the Intergaláctica that I first understood what the World Trade Organization was all about. The meeting was really the seedbed for Seattle.

Three years later, we were sitting in the streets of Seattle 60,000 strong, determined to disrupt the WTO's "millennial" round and I turned on either side of me and saw people who had been at the Intergaláctica.

Seattle was this killer rainbow of resistance. Steelworkers and rabbis, gays and nuns, longshoremen and people dressed like butterflies. And of course, the dread Black Bloc. They had to call out the National Guard to blot out the diversity. Seattle was a victory, one of the few. The Masters of the Universe had to call off the millennial round because we got between the convention center and the hotels where the delegates were staying. The tear gas was flying and it was too dangerous to transit the few blocks to where the meetings were being held and everyone went home pissed.

The nation born at Seattle dogged the WTO wherever it went, dogged the IMF and the World Bank, G-7 or G-8, and the Summit of the Americas. Wherever the "Death Merchants" tried to convene. Genoa, Mar del Plata, Prague, Hong Kong, Washington, Quebec City. One year, the G-8 had to meet north of Banff in a glorified hunting lodge. The population around the meeting site was so sparse that there were more grizzly bears than people in the neighborhood.

In 2003, the WTO came to Cancún for what was supposed to be the final meeting of the Doha round. Doha—after Seattle, the WTO had fled to Doha, Qatar, because no demonstrations are permitted there—was all about agricultural "trade," the rich nations of the North trying to pressure the South into opening up their markets to the dumping of obscenely subsidized agribiz products. In Japan at the time, every dairy cow was allotted $7.50 USD daily to sustain production—half of the world's population live on less than two bucks a day. That's obscene.

About 12,000 protesters showed up, mostly Mayan farmers from the Yucatán. There was a small international presence, including many Koreans. The Koreans made a dragon out of folded paper and put it in a stout wooden box. It was the Korean Day of the Dead, the farmer Lee Kyung-hae told me as we marched to the barricades. The Koreans tried to batter down the fence with the dragon and Mr. Lee hopped up on the box, climbed to the top of the barricade, pulled out a dagger and stabbed himself right in the heart. He was wearing a sign around his neck that said "WTO Kills Farmers!" He fell about ten feet from me.

Mr. Lee's suicide poisoned the WTO meeting. The subsidy thing drove off the poor countries and they went home. It was like tropical Seattle. I wrote the story up for the *Bay Guardian*, but here is the real story.

THE THREE DEATHS OF MISTER LEE

Mister Lee had some cows
But he lost them to the bank,
His friends explained sadly,
Sometimes Mister Lee
Would return to his lost farm
And just sit there
Staring at the fallow land
Blowing away in the salt wind.
Times are tough for small farmers
In Korea,
In India,
In Africa,
In Mexico,
In the south,
In the north,
The east, the west,
He had some land,
He had some cows,
He lost them both
To the bank or the bad government
Or the World Trade Organization,
Something bigger than himself.
That was Mister Lee's first death.

Mister Lee flew to Cancún Mexico
With several comrades
To protest against the WTO,

The banks,
The bad governments,
The something bigger than themselves.
They vowed to sweep them all
Onto History's garbage pile
And on the day of their dead,
The Korean farmers marched
Right up to the gates of the palace
And tried to batter them down
With folded dragons.
Mister Lee who was not
A young man anymore,
Climbed the barricade
And with a warrior cry,
Plunged the dagger
Deep into his heavy heart.
I saw him teeter and fall,
His tired blood
Spilling out upon the earth
As he merged with his ancestors.
That was Mister Lee's second death.

The day after Mister Lee's second death,
A handful of farmers
Wearing green kerchiefs
Brought candles and white flowers
To mourn Mister Lee
Right inside the belly of the beast,
They marched round and round
The Cancún Convention Center
Laden with their sadness,
So dignified by it
That their authority
Caused the officials of
The World Trade Organization
To flinch, an uncommon posture
For such great men.
Then the *campesinos*
Built an altar,
All candle wax and white petals,
To remember the lost land,
The lost cows,
The lost dreams,
The dead farmers
Spread under the blazing sun
North, south, east, west.

And on the second day

After Mister Lee's second death,
We danced in the street
And the Cancún police
Began to weep.

And on the third day
After Mister Lee's second death,
We pulled down the barricades
With thick, braided hawsers
And Chaac[7] rained down
On the green green ground
And we insisted to the Gods
That we were all Mister Lee.

And on the fourth day
After Mister Lee's second death,
The delegates from the poor place
In the south of Mama Earth's planet
Took Mister Lee into their hearts
And the talks collapsed into ashes
In the mouths of the powerful
And we all went home smiling.

That was Mister Lee's third death,
His resurrection and ascension
Into the lost lands
From which he would be born
Again and again.

Seven years after Seattle, the anti-globalization resistance spreads across borders, is inclusive and growing, a non-hierarchal thrust that works on issues not ideologies, confronts homogenization with creativity, puts its bodies on the line, and tells the story from the bottom up. It's no accident that Indymedia was born at Seattle.

III.

Globalization is a big story. Planetary in fact. Rebel reporters have to cut it down to bite-size wedges to be able to tell the story in digestible installments. A good place to begin as I said before is at your neighborhood store. Where does all this junk come from? We need to follow the trail.

Let's go back into Wal-Mart for a second. The homicide rate is soaring in Oakland. Our kids are getting whacked out here in the Mission. Where do the guns come from? Wal-Mart is America's largest legal gun seller. And where does Wal-Mart get its guns? From the Chinese People's Army, that's where.

A rebel reporter worth his or her salt would follow a local murder, maybe a friend even, back to where the story begins. *Ir al lugar de los hechos*. Find out what working conditions are like at Chinese People's Army gun factories, what the people are paid, how they live their lives. This would be a great anti-globalization story.

Globalization means there is always a global trail to follow. One of the first stories I did for the *San Francisco Examiner* when I worked at Pacific News Service looked at Mixtec Indian tomato pickers in the San Quentin valley south of Ensenada. They and the tomatoes they were picking were bathed in pesticides. Babies were dying. White guards—company goons—wouldn't let us into the camps to speak with the workers. Union organizers were killed. We followed the tomatoes. They were destined for California and Arizona McDonald's during the winter months. We wrote the series—it ran over three days. Sandy Close from Pacific News Service had some friends in Sacramento and a legislative hearing was held on a possible statewide boycott of San Quentin tomatoes. This never happened but we got a lot of ink. Remember, this was in 1984. Globalization wasn't even a word yet.

Getting legislation passed that would change these things is a feather in the cap of a rebel reporter. The only story I ever followed that did help get a law passed was about turtles, Pacific coast sea turtles. They were disappearing. In the late '80s, I followed the turtles down the Mexican coast from Mazatlán all the way to Mazunte, Oaxaca, where I reported on a turtle slaughterhouse. The turtles wept when the butchers bashed in their little skulls so now they shot them with .22s.

The story caught Earth Island Institute's eye and they put a picket line on the Mexican consulate in San Francisco. The picket line became a national boycott to which the Mexican government finally responded by passing a law against turtle egg poaching and posting the Navy on Pacific Coast beaches. Mazunte was shut down and became a turtle museum. Unfortunately, the poaching of sea turtle eggs and meat is still a thriving business.

In finding these stories and reporting on them, we follow the guiding principles of rebel investigative reporting: who is getting screwed, who is doing the screwing, how can those being screwed change this equation?

The first commandment of covering global resistance to globalization is to know thine enemy. Find out all you can about who they are. Know who is in charge, who controls those who are in charge, what cars they drive, where they live and what they eat. Know who is on the board of directors and what other crimes they have committed. Understand the nuts and bolts of the screwing, and how it works. Understand the law, the arcane language of trade pacts. Most of all, as our colleague Greg Palast never fails to admonish, follow the money as it moves from hand to hand, from corporate hitman up to the supreme capo. Always *ir al lugar de los hechos* and report the story from the bottom up.

Reporting global resistance to globalization from the battlefield—anti-globalization demonstrations—requires a hard hat. Independent reporters were beaten into the sidewalk like so many baby harp seals at the November 2003 Summit of the Americas in Miami, Florida. Covering these confrontations can be problematic. Everyone from Homeland Security to the Navy Seals are in on the act now. Globalphobes are practically put in the same bag these days as enemy combatants. They are potential terrorists. There are blacklists and mass arrests, and Guantánamo prison is probably next.

An early fork in the road in covering these battle royals is where you want to cover the action from. Getting accredited—the WTO and its associates like to accredit because it keeps reporters off the barricades—is a choice you have to make. A press credential means you will have access to seeing how power behaves in public and usually to a vast, whiz-bang press room where you can work shoulder to shoulder with the soldiers of the corporate press. But security and logistics at these global klatches is so tight that it is virtually impossible to both cover the barricades and also work inside. So you have to choose between basking in the rays of power or embedding yourself in the resistance.

Out on the barricades, do your best not to get isolated—hang with people. Don't carry a lot of fancy equipment—a mini-recorder, a digital camera if you must. I usually just fold up a sheet of blank paper and stick it in my back pocket, but I'm really low tech. If your equipment gets confiscated, protesters could be compromised. Ask Josh Wolf about that.

Getting the global resistance story, whether it's about sea turtles or dead languages or murder in the Mission, is not spot news. Following the trail takes months. You have to give yourself a big chunk of time. And getting the global resistance story is only getting half the story. Getting the story is one thing, getting the story out there is another. And you have an obligation to get this story out there, an *oficio*. You are part of the story now.

You have to write it, sell it, take it on the road. Put together a slide show, speak at universities, write a book based on your stories, turn your words into a campaign and a campaign into deeds. *Ir al lugar de los hechos* again and again. Take others with you. Stay in touch with those whose story it is. Be patient. The revolution does not come all at once. The revolution leaks all the time.

THE REVOLUTION IS NOT LIKE A FAUCET

The revolution doesn't begin
Over lattes at the Epicurean,
Does not begin with gravy and grits,
In the first joint, the last hit,
The morning *Chron*, your morning sh*t.
The revolution doesn't begin

Pulling greenchain on the graveyard shift
Or making the welfare line by nine,
The revolution doesn't begin
In your mind, your heart, your liver,
Your prick, doesn't begin
When you clench your fist,
The revolution doesn't begin
In 1776, 1917, the Depression, the dawn,
Doesn't begin with gurus, Cinques,
The news from L.A., Havana, *mañana*,
The revolution doesn't begin
With both barrels, on the pages
Of bibles, with the blues,
The revolution doesn't begin,
The revolution has no beginning,
The revolution is unending,
The revolution is not like a faucet,
The revolution leaks all the time,
You can't call a plumber to fix it.

Class dismissed.

Lecture Three

How to Be an Anti-War Correspondent

I.

On October 27, 2006, our colleague and *compañero de la lucha*, Brad Will, was gunned down while filming at a barricade in Oaxaca, Mexico, where a popular movement occupied the center of the city for months demanding the removal of a corrupt governor, Ulises Ruiz. Brad's killers are plainly visible on the last frames he shot—his camera kept filming even after he was down. Their red T-shirts identify them as Ulises's gun thugs, his death squads. Besides Brad, as many as 25 other participants in the popular movement have been murdered since May 2006.

Brad Will was self-assigned to Oaxaca for Indymedia. Brad had to go to Oaxaca. This was where the resistance was now. Brad Will fit the job description for a rebel reporter. He was covering a rebellion. His work would help to incite solidarity and further rebellion. By getting killed on the barricades, Brad became a participant in this rebellion.

I saw Brad in Chiapas when *La otra campaña (*the Other Campaign)[1] kicked off in January of 2006. He had previously covered conflicts in Brazil and Bolivia and we shop-talked for a minute. As a rebel reporter, Brad knew how to turn his words into deeds. He had nearly gotten killed at a demonstration of the landless in Brazil, had been a tree-sitter in Oregon. On Amy Goodman's show, *Democracy Now!*, on October 30, friends remembered him standing defiantly on the roof of a Lower East Side squat as the wrecking ball descended, in defense of a community garden as an autonomous space. Brad understood the Zapatista injunction: be a Zapatista where you live.

27

The good part of this tragedy, if there was a good part, was the solidarity of Brad's colleagues in the Mexican press. But the U.S. corporate correspondents didn't even consider him a reporter—he was an activist, a tree-sitter, yada, yada. Moreover, he was responsible for his own death because he reported from the protesters' side of the barricade in solidarity with the popular movement.

That's not to say Brad's death was ignored by the U.S. press. Even if he wasn't a reporter, Brad was a gringo. The attention paid to his murder was a measure of the racism of corporate correspondents in Mexico. Brad's name ran big, but the other 25 victims of Ulises's death squads were ignored.

Brad Will went to Oaxaca to cover what has become a dirty war but he was not a war correspondent. In pledging his life and his work to achieving peace by achieving justice, Brad Will became an anti-war correspondent. [2]

Brad Will! Live like him!

I really need to talk about how to be an anti-war correspondent and what that means. I suppose the prerequisite for doing that kind of work is to be anti-war.

II.

After George W. Bush sent a few boatloads of marines to Lebanon under the pretext of rescuing U.S. citizens trapped by the Israeli onslaught, [3] I had a flashback while marching around in front of the *Yanqui* embassy in Mexico City. Nearly 50 years before, almost at the same time of the year, in 1958, another U.S. president—Eisenhower was his name—had sent marines into Lebanon to back a fascist Falange regime. I got so incensed I tore up my draft card—my selective service registration—sent the pieces back to the draft board, and took off for Mexico. I suddenly realized that that was how I came to be where I was still living 50 years later, in Mexico.

I returned to the U.S. in 1964 to take part in the civil rights movement that was on fire all over the land. In San Francisco we sat in at the Sheraton Palace Hotel and up on Van Ness Auto Row. Hundreds went to jail weekly and I was arrested repeatedly. In those days, the FBI computers worked on molasses…

Here's how I tell it in *Murdered By Capitalism*:[4]

> The FBI computers worked like they were powered by molasses back in 1964 and it was a wonder they ever got their man. Finally, in April, the brown shoes surrounded the Zen house up on Mullen Avenue and knocked politely. Barton's wife Marty answered the door. She was nursing the baby and agent Ralph J. Fink (that's right—his name was Fink!) was embarrassed and said he would wait outside for me.

They took me down to the FBI headquarters for the obligatory grilling. Cool, I laughed, you can drive me to work—I had caught on with a sub-contractor janitoring at the old Federal Building and actually wiped off the FBI transoms every night. Jimmy, a little Muslim cat, and I had been systematically sabotaging the fortress-like premises for months, taking down portraits of President Lyndon Johnson, scrawling *Viva Fidel!* in red crayon on the back, and hanging them back up. We had also emptied the building of those annoying black and yellow nuclear attack shelter signs.

My bust was one of the first Vietnam draft beefs in the country. Even though my original objection had been to Eisenhower's invasion of Lebanon, that incursion didn't ring many bells by 1964. But by then I wasn't going to fight in any U.S. imperialist war wherever it was staged.

The army had no idea of who it was dealing with and cheerfully offered me one last chance to sign up to fight for the Free World against Godless Communism although I was now 26 and past draft age and the father of a family. I told them to go f*ck themselves and applied to Julian Bond at the Student Nonviolent Coordinating Committee in Atlanta for a job that would really be in the national interest...

In the end, I pled *nolo contendere* to refusing induction—I was proud of what I was doing and did not want to say I was not guilty. But I wasn't a pacifist—I fancied I would pick up the gun when it came to self-defense or national liberation...

I put on a big show at the sentencing. I read a statement in my pidgin Purépecha (the language of the Indians with whom we had lived for so long) about how the Vietnamese were not our enemies. I drove the judge batty by howling a few stanzas of Bob Dylan's "Masters of War." I read the Brecht poem "To Posterity," which says "Ah what an age it is / when to write of a tree / is a crime / because it is / a kind of silence / about injustice." I did everything but tap dance to get the judge's attention. Hizzoner, whose name has disappeared beneath the slagheap of trivia that calls itself my memory, wiped away a yawn and asked if I was done.

I caught two years, six months in the slammer and 18 months working in "the national interest" not at SNCC but scrubbing baseboards at Mt. Zion Hospital. The federal marshals snapped on the cuffs and chained me to a string of prisoners they were moving south. Whenever we got out of the car to piss along I-5, I rattled my chains energetically to the great annoyance of my fellow convicts. I wanted everyone to know I was a prisoner of LBJ's war.

The big gate at Terminal Island Federal penitentiary, San Pedro, California, clanked shut behind me. The date was August 3, 1964, the night before Johnson faked the Gulf of Tonkin incident to justify the bombing of North Vietnam. Later, LBJ had to go to congress to get a war powers act passed but the Gulf of Tonkin was where the war began. [5]

Despite its ominous name, Terminal Island was not really the end of the line. It was a medium-security lockup just outside L.A. with its share of celebrity prisoners. The mobster Mickey Cohen was one. There were a handful of political prisoners as well. The poet Maurice Ogden, whom the Feds framed for perjury after he signed a loyalty oath that said he was not now nor had he ever been a member of the Communist Party (he hadn't been either—he was a Trotskyist); Blackie Campbell, who had fought with the Canadian McKenzie-

Papineau Brigade in the Spanish Civil War and was doing his third bid for counterfeiting; Ben D., a black drug-runner who correctly argued that his crime had been a political one. Together, we formed the nucleus of the Convicts' Committee Against U.S. Intervention Everywhere.

Blackie taught me how to print leaflets on a bed of illicit gelatin he had smuggled out of the kitchen and the leaflets were my Waterloo. It was a felony to use federal writing paper to put out this garbage, the Warden bellowed at me. "I shed my blood for my country!" he frothed. "Well, I'm in your f*cking jail for mine," I counterpunched and they hammerlocked me off to the hole, the jail inside the jail, for a week.

Isolation was hard time. They kept the lights on me day and night and I began to lose track of where I was. I stayed sort of sane by repeating that mantra by Ho Chi Minh, the one that says "being chained / is a luxury / for which to compete / at least the chained / have a place to sleep."

Well, a lot of sh*t happened in jail—I got my jaw broke by a crazed government dentist who kept calling me a yellow draft-dodger. My parole officer, a bullet-headed skunk named Victor Urban, tried to get me shanked.

So my time got short and then it was done. I rolled up, laced on my free shoes, pocketed my Greyhound voucher north. The bullethead walked me out to the front gate. He didn't want to see me back there at Terminal Island. "Ross," he barked, "you never learned how to be a prisoner."

Hey, put that on my tombstone, folks! "He never learned how to be a prisoner."

III.

First an anti-war correspondent has to be against war but what kind of wars? All wars? Religious wars? Civil wars? Imperialist wars? Just Vietnam and Iraq? What about World War II? Would you have joined up to fight Hitler and the fascists for the U.S. capitalist class? What about the arms merchants? Aren't all wars fought for the profits of the arms merchants and the rest of the capitalist class? Aren't all wars imperialist wars? A big bully power invading and occupying a weaker nation to dominate their natural resources and markets?

What about revolutionary wars, revolutions, armed rebellions? Do people not have the right to fight back? To pick up the gun in their own defense? Is there such a thing as a just war?

Don't look at me. I don't have the answers. The depth of one's commitment to peace with justice is a personal decision.

The Zapatistas are an army, the Zapatista Army of National Liberation. They have guns and uniforms and they are soldiers. Subcomandante Marcos says, "We became soldiers so there will be no more soldiers." The Zapatistas call their war *la guerra contra el olvido*, the war against forgetting, which I have translated in my third book on the rebellion as the "War Against Oblivion," the obliteration of the past.

The Zapatistas say we are fighting the fourth world war, the war that globalization has declared against humanity. There are no fronts in this war. We are all its targets. "We did not ask for this war," they say, "but here it is and we have to defend our corn. *Ni modo.*"

Peace is not simply the absence of war nor is war simply the absence of peace. To be perfectly Orwellian, peace is war and war is peace. There is no peace without justice except the peace of the graveyard. People will fight back so long as there is injustice. Ergo we are always at war. Some call it the class war. Covering the class war greatly expands and confuses the definition of who is an anti-war correspondent.

Anti-war correspondents do not necessarily cover shooting wars, although they may get trapped in one. Sometimes we go in to try and stop wars before they begin. In 2003, I had the bright idea of riding up to Baghdad with hundreds of anti-war activists to try and stop America's crazed crusade before it began by placing our bodies between Bush's bombs and the Iraqi people. We called ourselves "human shields." Donald Rumsfeld said we were war criminals.

I had crossed the line from anti-war correspondent to anti-war activist, but still I am a reporter and I couldn't stop reporting. I wrote ten articles from Iraq for *La Jornada* in Mexico City on the eve of the invasion. It was really difficult to get them out. E-mail was heavily censored and sometimes I had to dictate them on the phone.

We didn't stop the war but, you know, the sites where we positioned ourselves—water treatment plants and electricity-generating facilities, a grain storehouse, and a refinery—all of them civilian infrastructure sites that had been bombed by the first Bush in 1991, did not get touched even though we had faxed off the geographical coordinates of each one to the White House. Maybe it was just G.W. Bush's bad aim.

Whether we stopped the war or not we made a connection. Going to Baghdad changed all of our lives. Here is a poem that I had the privilege to read at the Iraqi National Theater a week before the bombs starting falling.

THE OPEN VEINS OF THE PEOPLE

They will bloody the new moon
With their terrible daggers,
Blunt the horns
Of this luminous crescent
And rip open the night
That mother us all.
The killers will fall upon us
And all dreaming
Will be disallowed.
Only the screams

Of the skinned victims
Will be acceptable
In this brand-new
American nightmare.

We have come here
To this ancient land
To share with our blood
Brothers and sisters
The evisceration of hope.
We say that we will stand
Between the bombs of Bush
And the cradle of civilization
But indeed this is all metaphor
And pantomime. Now only
A god who died long ago
Can deconstruct the monsters
Who plan this genocide.

I am an old man
Who has lived
An honorable life
And now seeks
An honorable death
But I refuse above all
To surrender
My beating heart
To these whores of war.

Wherever my soul
Shall fly tomorrow,
It will never stop cursing
This bastard who calls himself Bush
And I shall survive
In the flowers of the desert
And the open veins of the people.

I guess what this poem teaches is that even if you are an anti-war correspondent covering a war you hate, you could well be killed in it so better be
prepared to depart this vale of tears at a moment's notice. Before I went off
to Baghdad, I wrote out a will and said my goodbyes. Death is an occasion-
al hazard.

Sometimes, anti-war correspondents go in after wars to describe the futil-
ity and the horror of war. In the spring of 1991, right after the first Bush
declared victory in the first Gulf War, I flew into Kuwait on a mission for the
Palestine Aid Society to report on the persecution of Palestinians in that
oilocracy in the wake of the war. Yasser Arafat had backed Saddam Hussein,

and Palestinians who had lived in Kuwait for generations were being vamped, arrested, tortured, and deported by the Al-Sabah dictatorship that had been restored by the *Yanquis*.

During my time there, I was invited to visit what the media had slugged "the Highway to Hell," the highway out of Kuwait City north to Basra—it was reportedly built by Arafat's construction company.

On the night of February 27 and 28, 1991, as tens of thousands were fleeing from the U.S. invaders, wave after wave of American warplanes stationed on carriers out in the Persian Gulf strafed and bombed the long lines of vehicles heading north, slaughtering Iraqi soldiers who had thrown down their weapons, in violation of the Geneva Accords—but also many civilians. The United Nations mission there told us 22,000 had been buried in common graves out in the desert. A pilot interviewed on CNN said it was "like shooting fish in a barrel." Twenty-two thousand! What happened on the Highway to Hell was an enormous war crime but no one even remembers this massacre today. The corporate media have disappeared it from memory. Abracadabra! How could this have happened?

By the time we got out to the highway, the desert was like a big parking lot jammed with charred vehicles. Everything, Iraqi army trucks, taxis, private cars, buses, even bicycles, was burnt to a crisp. Then the marines had come in and spray-painted "Saddam Sucks!" and sports slogans like "Go Redwings!"

We walked the shoulder of the highway and I saw a baby's car seat, a woman's high-heel shoe, books, evidence of civilian flight. The desert floor was covered with thousands of cluster bombs that drifted down on little parachutes like toys. The children picked them up and they blew off their faces. The cluster bombs were dropped by shells made from depleted uranium.

I had to maneuver carefully around the bomblets to retrieve this. Here, pass this around [Ross hands a book around to class]: it's the spoils of war. A book ironically entitled *The History of Victory*. Saddam's soldiers must have dropped it on the way out. Check out the inside of the cover. The desert has pressed itself into the page.

Anyway, I wrote the Highway to Hell story for the *Examiner*, but I guess I had too much to tell. My editor cut out half of it.

IV.

Brad Will was one of 85 journalists killed on the job in 2006, according to Reporters Without Borders,[6] 41 of them in Iraq. That's about 25% more than in 2005, when 64 ate it. In 2004 there was only one less death, but in 2003 it was only 43—almost the same number who were killed in Iraq alone in 2006.

The big surge in numbers is attributable to Iraq, the most dangerous place for reporters, rebels or not, to work on the planet today.[7]

Iraq is just the latest killing floor for news gatherers. When in doubt, shoot the messenger. Ninety-eight Argentine journalists died or were disappeared during the dirty war between 1976 and 1983.[8] Eighty-nine were killed in the wars in Salvador and Nicaragua from 1979 through 1989. Seventy-nine in Vietnam from '65 to '75, according to the Japanese Press Association. Because it lasted only five years (1993-1998), the fundamentalist uprising in Algeria was probably the most deadly war for reporters—58 were liquidated. Colombia is a hot spot—52 have been killed between 1988 and the 2006. So are the Philippines, Turkey, Sri Lanka, Bosnia, Kosovo, and Mexico, all of them in double digits.

The killing of ace investigative reporter Manuel Buendía on orders from the director of national security was the scandal of the 1980s in Mexico. According to the Committee to Protect Journalists (CPJ), 27 journalists have been killed in Mexico since 1992.[9] That number only includes those for whom the murder motive has been confirmed, attributed in most cases to crime and corruption. Most of the murders of Mexican journalists today are attributed to narco-gangs.

But Iraq is the killing field par excellence. The last count I had from CPJ was 85 dead since the U.S. invasion in March 2003 through 2006, including 11 Europeans and two U.S. citizens. Three were Arabs from countries other than Iraq, but the vast majority—64—were Iraqi. Forty-nine of the dead reporters were murdered outright and 36 killed in crossfires. As might be expected, 79 were men and six women. The toll includes 23 photographers, 49 reporters, and six producers. In addition, 35 media support workers (translators, drivers, and bodyguards) have also been killed in Iraq.[10]

The reason why so many Iraqi news workers have lost their lives in this cruel war is really a matter of dollars and cents. Iraq is too costly for U.S. "war correspondents." When an ABC anchor Bob Woodruff got blown up while embedded in a tank, ABC-Disney insurance costs for their correspondents went sky high. So the corporation hires proxies to get the actualities— the dusky natives are signed up for a pittance to get blown to smithereens. They get no bylines or screen credits and would probably be killed by the insurgents if they did. The bottom line is let the "wogs" get butchered. It's just corporate media racism as usual.

CPJ attributes 54 of the 85 journalists killed in Iraq to the insurgency, including six embedded reporters.[11] The U.S. has killed 14 news gatherers. I think of Mazen Dana, a valiant Palestinian photographer who survived the siege of Jenin and was gunned down by U.S. Army Rangers outside Abu Ghraib prison. They said they thought his camera was a weapon. An Arab with a camera? Bam! Bam! More racist bullsh*t.

CPJ insists that the U.S. military is not targeting reporters, but on April 8, 2003, a Bradley fighting vehicle crossing a bridge over the Tigris River stopped and turned its cannon on the Palestine Hotel a half mile away, where unembedded journalists in Baghdad were housed, and blew up the 15th floor. José Couso, a cameraman for Spain's Telecinco, and a Ukrainian working for Reuters were killed and several others were critically wounded. Couso's brother spoke at New College and showed footage of this deliberate assault. Hours before, the U.S. had bombed the offices of Al-Jazeera killing Tareq Ayoub. There are leaked transcripts of a Bush-Blair meeting in Washington that spring in which George W. Bush boasts of his intention to blow Al-Jazeera off the air. This looks like pretty deliberate targeting to me.

V.

From where do anti-war correspondents cover wars? From an armchair? On CNN? With a remote and a cell phone and a laptop at the ready? Wars are not really virtual, not really video games like the electronic media would want you to think. *Ir al lugar de los hechos.*

So from where? The battlefield? The home front? The battlefield is only part of the story. There are good anti-war stories on the home front—the anti-war movement, how the press reports these conflagrations. I covered Vietnam and the wars in Central America from the Mission District in San Francisco.

Vietnam came home hard in the Mission District. The two buildings where New College is now, were funeral homes. They sent those killed in action here for distribution to the hinterlands. Some of the coffins were sealed because the fathers and husbands and sons inside were in too many pieces for viewing. We took pictures of the flag-decked coffins stacked up on the sidewalk outside and published them every month in the revolutionary rag we were putting out, *Spark/Chispa.*

The Sandinista revolution in Nicaragua took place in the Mission District as well. As the Sandinistas surged, there would be meetings here every Saturday at the 24th Street BART plaza, which was rechristened "Plaza Sandino" in honor of the "Zapata of Nicaragua." There were many anti-Somoza refugees living in the Mission and the rallies spilled out into the street. Friends like Roberto Vargas, the poet, went off to fight on the Southern Front.

And the Salvadoran holocaust was all around us. It was in the Mission District with us every day of the bloodletting. San Francisco was a sanctuary city and the refugees poured in, some bearing fresh marks of torture. They were taken in at Most Holy Redeemer on 18th and Diamond. You went there and wrote their stories. The FMLN, the Salvadoran resistance, was very active in the Mission. Their storefront was just up the block on 20th and Valencia, where the *santería* shop is now. The war in El Salvador was all around us here.

VI.

Anti-war correspondents have to come up with various strategies for reporting wars. Stephen Crane was an anti-war correspondent in the U.S. Civil War and afterwards wrote a gruesome novel about it. Kids are assigned to read his *Red Badge of Courage* in high school English. That book has some of the grisliest scenes ever painted of war. Generations of American adolescents have been forced to read it. I think that's how I got turned on to this anti-war correspondent stuff.

So literature, songs, poetry are all strategies for reporting the horror of war. Here's how Carolyn Forché, a poet who worked for Amnesty International in El Salvador in the late 1970s, reported on that homicidal time:

THE COLONEL

What you have heard is true. I was in his house. His wife carried a tray of coffee and sugar. His daughter filed her nails, his son went out for the night. There were daily papers, pet dogs, a pistol on the cushion beside him. The moon swung bare on its black cord over the house. On the television was a cop show. It was in English. Broken bottles were embedded in the walls around the house to scoop the kneecaps from a man's legs or cut his hands to lace. On the windows there were gratings like those in liquor stores. We had dinner, rack of lamb, good wine, a gold bell was on the table for calling the maid. The maid brought green mangoes, salt, a type of bread. I was asked how I enjoyed the country. There was a brief commercial in Spanish. His wife took everything away. There was some talk of how difficult it had become to govern. The parrot said hello on the terrace. The Colonel told it to shut up and pushed himself from the table. My friend said to me with his eyes: say nothing. The Colonel returned with a sack used to bring groceries home. He spilled many human ears on the table. They were like dried peach halves. There is no other way to say this. He took one of the ears in his hand, shook it in our faces, dropped it into a water glass. It came alive there. I am tired of fooling around he said. As for the rights of anyone, tell your people they can go f*ck themselves. He swept the ears to the floor with his arm and held the last of his wine in the air. Something for your poetry, no? he said. Some of the ears on the floor caught this scrap of his voice. Some of the ears on the floor were pressed to the ground. [12]

Another strategy for anti-war correspondents: blogging. Now U.S. troops have access to the Internet and are blogging from the battlefield, unmasking that genocidal war for what it is worth. And the Iraqis are blogging like crazy too. Go to *IraqiGirl*[13] —she's 17 now but has been blogging from Iraq since the war began. It is like *The Diary of Anne Frank* for our time. And cell phones! Everyone's an anti-war correspondent now, a rebel press photographer. You don't have to graduate from some swank J-School to do this work. You just have to be against the war.

VII.

There are a few golden rules for covering conflicts. Keep your head down, watch your back, and be prepared for the worst. Do not wear a T-shirt that says *No Dispare! Soy Periodista!* (Don't Shoot! I'm a Journalist!). They were popular in El Salvador and my fearless colleague Mary Jo McConahay gave me one. I wore it during a demonstration in Santiago on May 1, 1986. Pinochet didn't like *periodistas*. The Chilean reporters I was with practically ripped it off my back. You're going to get us all killed, they explained.

Don't get embedded. Every major media working in Iraq is embedded. The correspondents stay holed up in their hotel rooms in the Green Zone and never move without a military escort. They ride around embedded in military convoys and never talk to anyone except the U.S. military. They don't do news. They do publicity blurbs for an invading army.

Anti-war correspondents do not embed. We do not ride into battle behind an occupying army. We are not part of the War Machine. Phil Sands who now strings for the *San Francisco Chronicle*, was with us in Baghdad, a nice young man who really wanted to cover the war from the ground up as an independent reporter. He tried it for a while and got kidnapped. It was pretty traumatic. He finally got away from his captors, but after that he decided to embed. But of course he could only get the wrong side of the story from that vantage point.

So now he reports the war from the refugee camps in Jordan. Refugee camps are excellent places from which to do anti-war correspondence. Everyone has a story to tell. Refugees know about these wars firsthand, probably better than anyone outside of the dead. They have survived.

Doing anti-war reporting from Iraq is a high-wire act. You have to either be fearless or a fool. I don't know how colleagues like Robert Fisk and Patrick Cockburn come through unscathed—the hand of God must be on their shoulders. Dahr Jamail's reportage from Fallujah was a daredevil mission. There's something to be said for the adrenaline of danger, the rush you get from going in on your own, knowing you could eat it at every step but doing it anyway. It gets to be a good drug.

Should anti-war correspondents fear for their lives? F*ck yes. I'm not dead yet, but I could have been any number of times. When that moment comes, it's kind of like you are inside a movie watching yourself from the outside. There's nothing you can do about it so just sit back and watch how it all turns out.

I have never been in a shooting war, the heat of battle like they say in the war movies, but I've had my share of close calls from men with guns. Not with any women. Yet.

One of those calls came during a street riot in Chile. In those days, I could still see enough to shoot photos of what I was covering, and I had a roll of the Santiago police opening fire on the leaders of the CUT (Unified Workers Central) that I needed to get to a friendly United Press International (UPI) reporter downtown who was always being bounced by Pinochet. The army was spreading out on the side streets and I raced around a corner right into the muzzle of one of those snub-nosed machine guns, an Uzi or an AR-15. I mean that little tab on top of the barrel actually got stuck up my nostril! It felt cold. My hands jerked up reflexively. The sergeant behind the gun screamed something at me I couldn't understand. But a higher power was with me—he either didn't have his finger on the trigger or the safety was on. My nose wasn't impaled and I slid myself off the barrel and began backing up to the corner—it was only four or five steps—and the gorilla didn't open fire. When I made it to the safety of the corner, I just collapsed on the sidewalk. I still had the roll of film clutched in my hand.

I was tracking an indigenous guerrilla group in the Cauca region of Colombia, Quintín Lame. Colombia is a dangerous place to do this work. I sat down in the outdoor *cantina* in a market town, Malongo, where I was to meet my contact and the waitress came and warned me that the last person who had sat there—just last night—had had his throat cut.

I needed to interview someone from Quintín Lame, and the contact kept insisting that he wasn't a member of the guerrillas although he probably was. It wasn't good enough. So we went down the road and talked to a truckdriver whose brother was a fighter. We drove up the hill and he f*cked up his pickup truck, which really pissed him off. We hiked up to the first camp and, of course, his brother wasn't there. A woman pointed straight up and so I began to climb for the second camp. It had started to rain. Our guide did not want to hike up the mountain so he pulled a .357 magnum from his waistband and started popping off all around me. He laughed that he was just shooting squirrels but I knew I was the next squirrel. So we went back and I didn't get the story although I had something. Better I figured to get that out than to be buried up there in a shallow grave in the Cauca where not even my editor knew I was prowling about. The rule of thumb is that dead reporters don't file. So I guess that's the moral. Make good decisions. Stay alive to file the story. That's part of your job, your *oficio*.

I'm telling war stories, not anti-war stories. In the end, it doesn't matter if we are for war or against it. We hate war, but we can't live without it. We are its whores.

I wrote this in Chiapas back in 2000 after the army and the police took down their checkpoints and we could finally travel freely in the zone. Everyone was talking about how peace was at hand. Holy moley, I was thinking. What are we going to do now?

WHORES OF WAR

In the houses
The tears have not dried yet.
They called him Manuel
Or Hugo
Or Ik,
The wind.
46 different ways
of saying dead
at Acteal. [14]
We list their names
In alphabetical order.
We count the sacrificed sheep
As we slip into numbing sleep.
Peace does not simply mean
The soldiers abandon the encampments
But that the camp becomes a *milpa*,
A corn field that again feeds
Those whose bellies
Never stop crying
For something to eat.
Peace does not still the nerve
That jumps for justice,
The absence of troops on the road
Or the death rattle of the overflights
Does not mean this war is done with.
War is half peristalsis,
Half *coraje*, wholly
A question of which hunger
Sustains us in the struggle
To sow the sky
With golden teeth of *maíz*,
A dream, the dream
Of dreaming without fear
Or tears, without
Waking up dead
With no one to mourn you.

Here in this sad beautiful land
We have witnessed a war,
It has made us a good living
Or just a living
But at least we are alive.
We have enumerated the crimes,
The victims, their surnames,
The circumstances
Of their maiming.
We have drunk deep
In the frozen nights
At the Casa Vieja Inn
To blot out the silences
Between assignments.
We love war.
We recoil at its horrors
But always find the words
To speak the unspeakable.
We are its whores.
Peace makes us feel
As if we have no place anymore
In a world that demands
Cruelty and credibility
All in the same breath and byte.
We file our stories
In a universe
That does not flinch.
We hear the sobs
Welling up from the ravines
And we shudder
Because we know
In the dark whorls
Of our corrupted souls
That there can never be peace
Outside of the boneyard.

We'll speak about language next week.

That will be the last class. Then you can go back to doing what you were doing before I interrupted you.

Lecture Four

Our Words Are Our Weapons:
The Language of Rebel Journalism

I.

Changing what we say.
Changing how we say it.
Listening hard.
Telling the tale.
Speaking in tongues.
Finding the phrase.
Saying what we want to say.
Ledes and kickers.
Tricking the reader.
The music of the news.
Our words are our weapons.
The longest poem.

That's the description in the syllabus for this final session "The Language of Rebel Journalism." If you know what all that means, you have a better handle on this than I have.

It's the fourth world war and our only weapons are our words. We need to keep our powder dry and our weapons clean and well oiled. Our words should be well chosen, that is, not just strung together from left to right but considered both for their accuracy and their music. Our words should be ready to paint the picture. They should be in technicolor and notice the sky and the wildflowers. They should be hard and concrete and not miss telling details. The writing is on the wall.

Our words should reach out and grab the reader by the throat or the eye or the heart. Our words should engage people. Most of all, our words should say what we want them to say. Language is alluring. It invites you up to her or his room and you fall into his or her arms and forget the point. Or maybe that is the point.

Rebel reporters use rebel language although not necessarily the language of rebellion, which is often frozen and formulaic and devoid of meaning. Rebel reporters are at war with clichés and the business-as-usual way of saying things. Rebel reporters do not make language into a business, a commodity to be bought and sold by the metric ton to the media mafias. Rebel reporters puke on the blandness of corporate journalism, the absence of passion.

"Two powerful car bombs ripped through a market in central Baghdad on Monday, turning an area crowded with shoppers into one of the worst scenes of carnage since the war began." See how the *New York Times* reporter quantifies the carnage? Rebel reporters cannot parse the horror.

"An American woman was killed on Sunday when her convoy of vehicles was ambushed minutes after she left a Sunni political party where she had been teaching a class on democracy." Although this lede tells you who, what, where, when, and how it doesn't tell you why. It leaves a lot of questions unanswered. Rebel reporters want to know why. Rebel reporters know they don't have all the answers.

This is how my colleagues in the corporate press are reporting the repression in Oaxaca: "President Calderón moved quickly to deflate a movement to oust the state governor that had turned violent as armed gangs and police fought protesters. While there has been no resolution to the conflict, the calm there prompted the U.S. State Department to downplay tourist travel advisories." Here the reporter—it's an Associated Press story that appeared in the Mexico City edition of the *Miami Herald*—is shamelessly shilling for the tourist industry. She is looking at this story from above, not from the street.

AP reporters are as anonymous as their prose. The Associated Press is a big player in the lie machine. They get the story up first and that's what gets carried and becomes the official record. When López Obrador was pulling in millions to his meetings, AP reporter Mark Stevenson was deliberately playing down the numbers. I finally figured out why. Mark would leave the rallies early and get the story out first and never got an accurate count or even called the police for their estimate. His count was sometimes off by a million marchers and had the effect of diminishing the importance of the movement. Nonetheless, his numbers were what people remembered and even Amy Goodman on *Democracy Now!* was using them. We had an on-air chat about that one morning.

This is what I saw during a swing through Oaxaca at the same time the Associated Press Oaxaca story ran:

The walls of this city of painters have been freshly whitewashed on orders from a much-lampooned governor and financed by transnational tourist moguls. Neat squares of blankness cancel out the visual rebellion that exploded on the streets of this colonial city during seven months of intense skirmishing between the Oaxaca Popular People's Assembly (APPO) and striking teachers, and security forces backing Governor Ulises Ruiz whose separation from office the protesters demand.

Despite the ferocious repression—hundreds were arrested and 19 killed by Ruiz's death squads—an observer who keeps an ear to the ground and an eye on the whitewashed walls once plastered with revolutionary slogans and tags, murals, throw-ups, and ingenious stencils, realizes that the Oaxaca Intifada is hardly done with yet.[1]

It's not just the skew of these two visions of the Oaxaca resistance—the AP views it from the tourist industry's side of the barricade and I look at it from the popular movement's—but the language is distinct. The Associated Press flattens out the story, literally drains it of blood and color—Oaxaca is one of the most colorful places in Mexico.

Rebel reporters are storytellers. The narrative is what keeps the reportage moving. Sure, you want to weave in the facts and stats but the seamlessness of the narrative comes first, drawing the reader in and on. It's like when we were kids and someone's uncle told us a ghost story and we'd be on the edge of our seats almost afraid to find out what came next. That's my paradigm for a good story.

Rebel reporters are all Joe Hills, trouble-making troubadours moving from town to town singing out the news in public plazas. The emphasis is on singing here. Rebel reporters put the music in the news.

Rebel reporters cry out the news like the newsboys of yore. Extra Extra! Read all about it! Rumsfeld Crumbles Into Dust! Many years ago, I had a golden opportunity to do just that, walk around town and shout out the headlines. Vince, the old guy who usually sold the *Times Standard*, a Thomson chain rag, in Arcata, California, was dispatched to the county fair to hawk the paper at the racetrack for a week and asked me to cover his route. The timing was terrific. Richard Nixon was being forced to abandon the White House and I walked around Arcata shouting out the news. "Your President Is a Crook!" "Lights Out at the White House!" "Nixon Jailed on Alcatraz!" I did this until the local gendarmes fell upon me, hogtied my hands behind my back, and hauled me off to the hoosegow for disturbing the peace. So what if it was 3 o'clock in the morning? I was selling the early bird edition.

Rebel reporters are painters. We just don't write "the Zapatistas control an autonomous region in southeastern Chiapas." We paint it.

This Is What Autonomy Looks Like. Eyes, Many many eyes. Dark x-ray eyes, laser eyes, framed by black ski masks. Eyes on the walls of the rebel schools, the cooperative stores, the liberation chapels, the free clinics, the House of Good Government, the tortilla factories. Everywhere a wall. Every wall brimful of eyes. The penetrating stare of Votan Zapata,[2] of Francisco Villa, and the old anarchist Flores Magón. Zapatista eyes, rebel eyes, ancient eyes, newborn eyes, staring out at you from the walls staring into their eyes. A *caracol* of eyes. This is the Zapatista vision.[3]

This is not an art review. There are 400 murals in the Zapatista zone and they tell the story of this rebellion over and over again as you move from one community to the next.

Rebel reporters are *cronistas*. They keep the chronicles of events, the daybook. They tell you what came before and what could happen next. History permeates their writing. Rebel reporters cannot forget. Rebel reporters fight against amnesia.

Coming down from
The green muddy mountain
Where the *gringos* had gone
To build with the Zapatistas
The autonomous rebel highschool
Shovel by shovel and grain by grain,
The *chileno* photographer
Began to tell me how
His father had been tortured to death
By Pinochet's fascists, how they
Had broken his own ribs, his legs,
Hot-wired his testicles
And touched him tenderly
With lighted cigarettes,
They learned their techniques
From the *pinche* Nazis
He said matter-of-factly,
Whipping around the hairpin turns,
The dark spider of a storm
Brooding over the Valley of Jovel
Like the memory of what was to come.

In Lima over pisco sours,
Samuel told me of the 14 lost years
He left in prison,
He was a Tupamaro,
Would be one until his final breath,
There was nothing else he could be
After they took everything else away.
14 years, his hair turned white,

They beat him at first with hoses,
The darkness closed in,
There was nothing to read,
His family stopped coming one by one,
He survived only because
He was a Tupamaro,
Because he remembered
What that meant
Even if remembering
Is against the law
In Uruguay, in Chile,
It is official,
There is no memory,
You are not allowed
To remember the bad times,
They are over,
And the rememberers
Have been ordered
By the Commissions of Oblivion
To forget.

Juan Gelman refuses to forget.
They took his son, his daughter-in-law,
His soon-to-be-born grandchild.
All the way down to the Zapatista convention
He told of his long search,
Recorded in a thousand sleepless nights,
A thousand poems that can never rest
Until his unborn grandchild is found.
It is official now in Argentina too,
This forgetfulness,
It is forbidden to remember
Who it is you are looking for
But Juan Gelman will never let go,
We are their memory he turns to me,
If we forgot them now
Then those who have been taken
Will never have existed.

In my own country,
Amnesia is the norm.
The schools teach us
To unremember from birth
The slave takings, the rising up,
The songs of resistance,
The first May First,
Our martyrs from the Haymarket
To Attica to the redwoods of California,

Ripped whole from our hearts,
Erased from official memory.
When we die
There will be no trace.

Here too in these green hills,
In the free Zapatista territories
Of Oventik and Polhó,
They will try and make us forget
The mass graves,
The babies ripped from the wombs,
The wounded families and villages,
The languages they spoke,
They will shrug and say
It never happened,
It is written nowhere,
No pasa nada aquí señor,
They will dig up the bones
And pound them down to powder
And lose the powder
In the four winds
But like Juan Gelman, Samuel, the rest
The Indians will never give up,
Will never abandon the memory of their dead
Never leave the past behind
Because the past will never go away,
The past is like a boomerang,
It will always return,
It is always present,
It is always future,
It is the most fundamental human right—
Memoria!
What belongs to us all.

That's from a chapbook, *Against Amnesia*. I wrote it after the massacre of 45 Tzotzil Indians in the Chiapas highlands at Christmas 1997.[4] Some things have changed since I wrote it. Juan Gelman found his granddaughter. Argentina, Chile, and Uruguay have begun to examine that terrible time.

Rebel reporters are, as you may have surmised, poets. We hear the music in the story. We cover the most mind-numbing events—political speeches, congressional sessions—but around the perimeters of these stories a poem is always lurking. I think of them as the out-takes.

Poetry enriches and infuses my vision. It has made me a better reporter and given me an edge over the corporate competition. It has helped me to notice stuff that I might miss in the rush of doing the news.

This is an out-take of a story I did in 2004 on transnational mining in Peru and how it is leveling the Andes. You see whole mountains blown away;

huge cyanide stains on the sides of the hills, people living in misery under the slagheaps and the toxic fumes of the smelters. Gold was up to $500 an ounce when I made this trip. I wrote this coming down from Cerro de Pasco, a gigantic strip mine 15,000 feet up in the sky. It's really just a list of the transnationals posted along the road down to Lima, what you call a serial poem.

>Down downhill
>Down to the bottom
>Suicide Curve
>Inca Kola
>La Oraya
>Smelter spewing
>Suicide poisons,
>Aranco
>Anglo-American
>Sullair
>Mitsubishi
>Transnational toxins
>Logos oh so proud
>To gouge down
>This mountain
>With our man-eating
>Machines
>Tajo eating up
>Pasco city
>Gobbling up
>The groundwater
>Vulcan
>Brocal
>Billeton
>Tierra Linda
>Communities
>In misery
>Ragged kids
>Mom thin
>As a tube
>Of dynamite
>By the roadside
>Arsenic
>Cyanide
>Fábrica de Carburos
>Yaltayaco
>Yanacocha
>Quillish Hill
>Newmont Mines
>The Montaro River
>*Cuidado*

Buenaventura Limited
Cuidado
Tambogrande
Cuidado,
Conacami is coming
In Quechua
In Aymara
Indígena
Inca Cola
Slow
Stripmine ahead
Slow
Stripmine behind
Slow
Dead condors above
Despacio
No
Peligro
No
Cerro de Pasco mining company
Mine Sur
Southern Peru Limited
Vista Gold International
Down
Downhill
Down to Lima
At the bottom
Danger
You are now entering
Jesus said
Believe in me
Suicide curve
And you shall be
Inca Cola.

II.

Being a poet lets me vent my outrage at the particular horror I happen to be covering. Helps me to find colorful ways of saying we have to stop this f*cking sh*t.

In 2005, I flew into Istanbul for the final session of the war crimes tribunal that had been convened to adjudge U.S. atrocities in Iraq. I delivered a paper on "greencard marines," young undocumented Mexican workers who had been tricked into joining the military and later killed in Iraq. There are over hundred now. My reporting from the tribunal was sober compared to the outrage that I felt. So this is the out-take.

TRIBUNAL

We emerge from hours
Days of hours
Hours of minutes
Minutes of seconds
Entombed in darkness
So heavily freighted
With the corpses
Of a hundred thousand Iraqis
That we cannot breathe
A cavern of horrors
This war
It is with us every second
Of every minute
Of every hour
This war
Weighing like a coffin
Upon our pierced hearts
Blindfolding us
Before the torturers
This war
They attach the cables
To our genitals
Jam them up our rectums
Searing us
With jolt after jolt
Of their imperial
Power tools
This war
We are beaten with rods
With chains, with each other
This war
Our minds are scooped out
By American monkeys
Wielding stainless steel spoons
This war
The noise of the rendering
Pummels our eardrums
This war
We watch our loved ones
Drawn and quartered
Forced to fake f*ck each other
In the drizzling gloom
Upon Bush's murder machine
Until our twisted lacerated
Corpses can no longer
Feel the sensation

Or taste the pain of
This war
We are frozen
In cryogenic darkness
From which we are
Only allowed to emerge
Drained and punctured
On the third day
After the crucifixion
Resurrected by our rage
This war
And then suddenly
As if nothing happened
Really
As if it was just one more
Bad dream
Really
We are in stunning sunlight
Above the azure sea
Watching the ferries
Drift off to Asia
The memory of
This war
A black blot
On the back of the brain
Like a paralyzing migraine
That will never go away

This war
This war
This war

From a kid on up, I was a newspaper freak. My pop worked at a New York daily and my mom was a publicist and her job was to get her clients' names in newspapers. We read eight daily newspapers in our home—five in the morning and three in the afternoon. The roster includes the *Daily Worker*, which arrived on her doorstep each morning.

I've always been addicted to stories that wittingly or not seem to be found poems. Here is one I found in the *Jerusalem Weekly*, an English-language Palestinian paper that is a good source for looking at Palestine as a nation state—I mean it reports on the Palestinian stock market and prospects for the Palestinian tourist economy. This story from Jenin appeared practically as it is written in this poem:

A PIECE OF CHOCOLATE

The three youngest boys
Begged their father
For just one shekel
To buy chocolate
From the market
But Abu Aziz was reluctant
To let them outside
The small house so late
In the afternoon
Still the curfew
Had been lifted in Jenin
And the market was
Only fifty meters away.
Besides they were good boys
Who always obeyed their parents
And never threw stones
At the soldiers of the Occupation.
So I gave them each one shekel
A shekel for Achmed
A shekel for Jamal
A shekel for Tariq
And told them
To hurry back home.

After just a few minutes
We heard a loud explosion
And feared for the worst.
A single Israeli tank
Stood smirking in the street.
You could still smell the smoke
From its terrible cannon
And we saw the boys then
Lying there in a heap.
Achmed's internal organs
Were spread all about them
On the ground
And Jamal's legs
Were cut in two.
Only Tariq was untouched
By the exploding shell.
When we ran to them
We saw that the boys
Were still holding
The piece of chocolate
In their little hands.

Both my sons died later
At the Doctor Sulieman Hospital
And we buried the two brothers
Still with the chocolate
In their hands.

So this is what it means
To be born a child
In Palestine these days.
You will die in the street
With a piece of chocolate
In your hand
And you will never
Get to eat it.

III.

Rebel reporters have to listen closely not only to what people are telling them but to how they are telling it. You must remember that these people are entrusting you with their story. You have an obligation, an *oficio*, to retell it in their words but also to translate through their words the who-ness of the person who is telling you the story. How do we capture this who-ness?

Everyone talks distinctly. The accents and the breaths rise and fall in different rhythms. Some speak softly, some bellow. Some speak with their hands. Do not forget to include the gestures when you record what they are saying. Many will speak in metaphors and idioms and with regional accents. By distinguishing voices in your stories you color in the who-ness of the person whose story it is. This helps the story to live. Rebel reporters cherish the uniqueness of persons in struggle and the commonalities of people who fight for change.

Rebel reporters have a rock-bottom responsibility to protect those who entrust us with their stories from the retaliation of their government or whoever it is that is screwing them. Those who place themselves in jeopardy because they've talked to me always wind up anonymous or with a "not-his-or-her-real name" in my stories. Rebel reporters follow Josh Wolf's example and don't give up their sources.

This injunction is kind of built into my genes. My mom was part of the Joint Anti-Fascist War Relief Committee in the 1940s. They helped refugees from the Spanish Civil War. The Senate Internal Security Committee's Pat McCarran wanted the names of the refugees, many of whom were Communists, but the committee wouldn't give them up. My mom went to jail for three months for contempt of Congress. It made me proud.

Rebel reporters need to listen hard to what the merchants of death are saying too. We have to open our ears to them and hear how they pitch their poison word for word—it is corroborating evidence. In the arrogance of power, they often spill the beans. They, like their victims, also speak distinctly, cast their language from their sleazy skew. We may not want to waste our time listening to their lies but we have to describe the way they tell them.

I've made it into an obsession to run away from covering power. The few times I've actually been present at a presidential press conference in the country where I work, I've been conspicuously snubbed when I raised my hand to ask an embarrassing question. You only learn what they want you to learn at these séances anyway. Even if you are invited, you are not obliged to attend.

Nonetheless, I've had a few weird and revealing interviews with presidents.

In 1988, soon after Carlos Salinas had stolen the presidential election—the computer system "crashed" on election night, and when it came back up 10 days later, he was declared the winner over leftist Cuauhtémoc Cárdenas—the new president came downtown for a flag-raising and wound up breakfasting at my local café. The place was crawling with cops and bodyguards and I pushed my way through the press mob to my usual stool at the counter. Then Salinas, having polished off his *huevos rancheros*, decided to visit the kitchen crew, a democratic enough gesture. As he emerged back into the dining area, I swung around on my stool and extended a hand. "*Señor Presidente!*" I saluted, pressing his hand and drawing him to me so that I could see the whites of his eyes. "Everyone in Mexico says you stole the election from Cárdenas. Did you steal the election, *Señor Presidente?*" I inquired. No one had ever asked Salinas this question to his face. The panic in the little man's eyes was almost poignant. By now his *guaruras*—bodyguards—were closing in to rescue him from my grasp so I released his hand and returned to my *café con leche*, totally jazzed because I had indeed just gotten an exclusive interview with the *Presidente*.

How I came to interview Bill Clinton was another story. This one was datelined right here in the Mish. In 1992, Clinton was running hard and he liked to do photo ops in ethnic neighborhoods so his people set up a meeting at 24th and Mission by the BART station, Plaza Sandino to us old-timers. A convoy of limos chugged in from the airport I suppose and a bunch of suits piled out. The Mission cops and the Secret Service had cordoned off the plaza but there weren't enough Democratic Party shills out there to fill out the photo and they invited in the uninvited. Immediately, I began shouting questions at Bubba—What about the Israeli loans? Where did he stand on NAFTA, the death knell for the *campesinos* of Mexico? Clinton appealed to his faithful—had they come out to listen to him or to me? Next thing I knew two Secret Service agents had bellied me to the edge of the crowd, clapped on the cuffs, and thrown me down by the top of the BART station stairs. They left me there until Clinton had finished his spiel. Then the suits got back into their limos and drove downtown for some fundraiser and the *Secretos* cut off the handcuffs and handed me a slip that said I had been detained for reasons of "public safety." We published the detention slip in the *Anderson Valley Advertiser* the next week. That was my interview with Bill Clinton.

I don't do interviews much anymore, least of all with presidents. Instead I try and talk with people one to one, *platicar* or *charlar*. There's a lot more give and take than in "interviews." One of the few advantages of getting old and decrepit is that I can talk with old people—we have common issues. This really came in handy during the post-electoral protests in Mexico City. So many of López Obrador's supporters were like they say "of an age," and they were a fertile source of both context and quotes.

I see the corporate reporters show up at these events with all their fancy equipment and shove a mic in someone's face. It's intimidating when the reporter whips out a mic or a steno pad and starts firing questions at the poor person they've pounced on. It's like "I'm asking the questions around here." The corporate press speaks from arrogance and power. It's really self-defeating because they never get the story right. People tell you what they think you want to hear. The reporter asks loaded questions and puts words in their mouth. No matter how laid back you are, people will talk differently with a tape recorder in their nose. They don't say what's in their heart with a camcorder trained on them. Back off.

I don't hardly use a tape recorder anymore and when I do it's just one of those Walgreen jobbies. I don't really care about the sound quality. If I carry a steno pad, it's always wedged down the back of my pants so that I'm not branded a reporter the moment I show up. Mostly, I've taken to folding up a sheet of paper and sticking it in my back pocket. Note taking isn't what it's cracked up to be anyway. You don't get everything. It's really like drawing a sketch of what someone is saying. You are so busy taking notes that you don't get to look your responder in the eye. You miss what's behind the words.

So how do we get it all down—what people said, how they said it, the smell, the colors of the story? You know, it's always being recorded right here. [Ross taps on his head.] Other stuff gets in the way and it gets erased if one doesn't stay really focused. Usually, I'll pull out whatever I'm taking notes on—my phone bill or an old leaflet—as soon after I've schmoozed up a responder as I'm able to, and get the key words down. I'll do a self-debriefing right away. Remembering the sequence is important—the key words will trigger the reconstruction of the interview.

I'm not a digital guy, but bad as my eyes are—the Mission District cops got my left one—they do function as my own inner digital camera. Rebel reporters view their stories frame by frame, trap the images in words, move onto the next frame. Making your eyes into a camera really puts you in the story. When I did pictures, I tended to put what I was seeing, my vision and my powers of description, on hold because I thought I had it all inside the camera. Cameras made me lazy.

Rebel reporters are travel writers. They notice the land and its contours and what grows there. They notice the desert light, the clearcuts, the rocks, the seasons. So many of the stories that we do are stories of place, of the defense of that place—the Lacandón jungle or a Nahuat sacred site, a mountain aquifer about to be sucked dry by the Coca-Cola Corporation of Atlanta, Georgia. We are obliged to put the place in the story and the story in its place. We need to locate that place, how it connects up with other places, the geography of struggle. We have to be cartographers.

Finally, rebel reporters construct their stories on context. How far back you want to go to set a story in context is optional but I must warn you that context eats up a lot of bytes. Too often, I've begun a story back in the days of the Conquest, 1492, 1519. It's a long way back to the point of the story.

Once I complained to a famous Mexican historian that my stories were running really long because I had to deal with so much context. The *maestro* patted me on the shoulder to calm my anxieties. "John, when a correspondent has been anywhere longer than ten years, he becomes an historian," he laughed. Sometimes I feel as if I am being crushed by the weight of history.

IV.

I promised you some tricks. How to hook in your readers and how to let them go—yeah, rebel reporters will resort to tricks if it helps to get their stories read. If you don't hook the reader in the first paragraph, the first sentence, the lede, your story dies and goes out with the recycling in the morning. So the lede is crucial, where you start the story. I always start my stories at the bottom and work them up to power. It was a cardinal rule at Pacific News Service, where I learned the ropes of this *oficio*, to start your story in the street.

An effective lede zooms in on a single frame, paints the place, colors in the faces, tells a second of their story, and encapsulates the injustice about to be revealed in the body of the story. Who gets screwed, who's doing the screwing? All of this must be accomplished in about 100 words, or else your editor will automatically dismember the lede and reduce it to the usual what-when-where-how formula. So my advice is to write tight.

Kickers are the other side of the money. They are a test of your readers' endurance. Will they stay with you until the bitter end? Kickers don't have to be the end, the last word. Kickers sum up the story, but you want to leave the readers to draw their own conclusions. Kickers flow from the logic of the text, but they should be sort of unexpected. They are what you leave the reader with. They are like making a graceful exit and leaving the reader asking who was that masked man?

Kickers can bring stories full circle. I just cranked one out on the privatization of *La Migra*'s detention facilities—how big corporations are making a bundle on the misery of migrants. The so-called corrections industry's portfolio is booming as what's now called ICE—Immigration and Customs Enforcement, a wholly owned subsidiary of Homeland Security—detains more and more undocumented workers.

I began the story in Chiapas and followed an old rusty bus crammed full of Indian farmers all the way to the northern border. My source told me how his brother had tried to walk across the desert and got busted and wound up in the Florence, Arizona, privately run detention center.

Bottom-line providers are contracted for food and health services in these centers. Even transportation has been privatized—AeroMéxico made $13 million in 2005 on contracts to fly "voluntary departures" back into the interior of Mexico far enough away from the border that they are discouraged to try and cross again. My friend's brother had just been flown back to Chiapas courtesy of AeroMéxico/Homeland Security. When he told me that, I knew I had a kicker.

Rebel reporters are always in their stories. They are embedded in them. You can't get out of your story so you have to write it from the inside out. Sometimes you will even wind up being a character in your story. There will be no other way to tell it.

I'm always showing up in mine, identified as "this reporter" or "a U.S. reporter"—it's a pretty cheesy way of getting involved. The "I" of me seems to show up only when I've been personally attacked or beaten or am feeling particularly martyred.

There are times when you are not just in the story, but you are the subject of it. Years ago, I found myself on a desolate stretch of Hunters Point on my way to Double Rock to purchase some herb which in those bad old days was sold in $20 matchboxes. I had my bucks tucked away where no one was going to take it off me and when two enterprising young men from the neighborhood decided to mug the white guy they couldn't find it. Furious, one of the muggers reared back his foot above me—I was already down on the ground—and kicked my nose in. "Take that, nigger!" I remember him as laughing. It was an epiphany—a nigger is the guy on the ground getting his nose bashed in.

Anyway, I got out of there alive, checked into Emergency at San Francisco General Hospital to have my nose reset, and went home and wrote it up for the California Living section of the *Examiner*, which bought it for $150. I was right there in the middle of that story and I actually made some money by being mugged.

I suspect that vignette is sort of a metaphor for doing this work. One of the few ways a rebel reporter is going to make a buck is by getting mugged. And you will be mugged a lot in this *oficio* by cops and crooks and editors and your J-School colleagues. People will misunderstand your intentions and whack the crap out of you and you wind up with chump change for your pain. There must be some other reward.

The coin of our realm is passion. While corporate journalists bask in the bland neutrality of their vaunted "objectivity," dabbling in a language drained of all outrage for fear of damaging their career track, rebel reporters, who know only too well they have no careers but rather a responsibility, are paid off in passion—passion for language, passion for telling the story with passion, passion for struggle and change, for sharing spirit, solidarity.

> And my veins do not end in me
> But in the unanimous blood
> Of all those who struggle
> For love
> For life
> For the things
> The countryside and the bread
> The poetry of everyone.[5]

So am I pissed off by capitalism, racism, sexism, classism, ageism, youthism, Stalinism, fascism, chauvinism, any ism? Do I think that another world is possible?

> Yes and I say Yes,
> Yes in light and Yes in peace,
> Yes in was and Yes it is,
> Yes with drums,
> Yes with gongs,
> Yes with flutes,
> With air, Yes
> Yes the Celestial,
> Yes the Master,
> Yes the Word,
> The Midnight Yes,
> The lugubrious Yes,
> The low-down Yes,
> The Yes meaning Yes,
> The elemental Yes,
> The Eternal Yo,
> The Wow, the Yow,
> The You, the Me,
> The Ouiouioui
> The SiSiSi

The YahYahYah
The YupYupYup
Yes and I say Yes

Oh yeah. Oh yeah.

F I N

Photos and Illustrations

Original Artwork by Lester Doré

EL MONSTRUO

The Monstruo is forever on the brink of simultaneous disasters. We are surrounded by 34 volcanoes, and monster earthquakes tremble beneath our feet. It has always been that way in this dangerous geography. The Aztecs sacrificed hundreds of thousands so that the gods would be pleased and not throw them out of this place. The struggle of Chilangos against the dire conditions that their physical environment imposes on them is the true story of this city.

Cities themselves are a kind of biblical curse. Cain slew Abel and built the first city. But urban catastrophe is our bread and butter, and even if all the walls fall down tomorrow, there will still be a city here. In the end, the Monstruo is the people who have lived in this place and built it up over and over again, millennium after millennium, each time angry gods or natural disaster or foreign conquest or revolutions have torn it down. Us Chilangos have clung to this complicated birthright as steadfastly as the stones upon which our Monstruo stands, and like the stones, we are here to stay.

Text from *El Monstruo: Dread and Redemption in Mexico City, by John Ross* © 2009. Illustrations by Lester Doré and José Guadalupe Posada. Printing by Flying Rabbit Press, Madison, Wisconsin.

El Monstruo, 2010, broadside printed on cream colored paper 35cm x 35cm. Text by John Ross, engraving on HDPE by Lester Doré, printed by Kate Clapper of Flying Rabbit Press, Madison, Wisconsin on a Vandercook S15 proofing press using Mohawk Superfine Text. The edition of 100 was signed by the author and the artist. The text is from the last paragraph of John Ross's book of the same title. This broadside was created to mark the occasion of Ross's 2010 visit to Madison. John Ross is shown as a *calavera* draped in his trademark Palestinian *keffiyeh*, his vest, and his beret, eerily foreshadowing his death less than a year afterward. Behind him rises then-president Felipe Calderón as a snake, dwelling among the buildings still leaning from the earthquake that brought Ross to the city, first as a reporter and then as a resident, in 1985. Creeping out of the ruins on spider's legs is Carlos Slim, the richest man in México and perhaps in the world, just behind a Roman Catholic prelate moving with the speed of a snail, while an ordinary *Chilango* crawls into the nightmarish traffic on the *Segundo Piso* of the Periférico expressway, an incomplete and inadequate attempt to facilitate travel by car across El Monstruo.

LA VIDA HEROICA DE
PRÁXIDES G. GUERRERO

TIERRA Y

LIBERTAD

The Life of Praxides G. Guerrero

"A fitful breeze
Blows through
Palaces and dungeons
Stables and cantinas
Factories and barracks
The academies of assassination
The breath of the Revolution!"

The Death of Praxides G. Guerrero

A sudden shot
In the red dawn
He does not see the bala ciega
La yegua rears and bolts
He tumbles from the saddle
The weeping of the Adelitas.

The Bones of Praxides G. Guerrero

A bronze bust
Paid for by
The state he hated
In the dusty boneyard
Of Janos Chihuahua
Sweet sugar cranios
A grinning calaca
Dancing with fierce abandon
On la Noche de los Muertos.

Que Muere el Mal Gobierno!
Que Viva Praxides G. Guerrero!
Que Viva la Revolución Mexicana!

John Ross

Illustration by Lester Doré • Printing by Kate Clapper, Flying Rabbit Press, Madison, Wisconsin

La Vida Heroica de Práxedis G. Guerrero, 2010, broadside printed on cream colored paper 43 x 35 cm. Poem by John Ross, engraving on HDPE and typography by Lester Doré, printed on letterpress by Kate Clapper at Flying Rabbit Press, Madison, Wisconsin in an edition of 100, signed and numbered by the author and the artist. The broadside is a companion to the *El Monstruo* broadside. Ross's poem is an ode celebrating the life and death of Guerrero, an associate of the anarchist revolutionary theorist and leader Enrique Flores Magón. Guerrero, a young intellectual, contributed articles to Magón's influential newspaper, *Regeneración*. (The name is in use again for a publication put out by contemporary young anarchists.) Guerrero organized a force of armed revolutionaries in El Paso, Texas, and led them across the border to begin one of the first armed struggles in the Mexican Revolution of 1910. He was killed the day after his troops captured the town of Janos, Chihuahua. The illustration, utilizing the style popularized by the great Mexican popular artist José Guadalupe Posada, depicts Guerrero dancing on the grave of Porfirio Díaz with Emma Goldman, the famous U.S. anarchist who had visited the Magonistas in El Paso. Flores Magón, on accordion, and a guitar-playing *adelita*, as the women who fought on side of the revolution were known, provides the music.

LA VIDA HEROICA DE
PRAXEDIS G. GUERRERO

La vida de Práxedis G. Guerrero

"Sopla una brisa intermitente
Através de los palacios y mazmorras
Los establos y las cantinas
Las fábricas y los cuarteles
Las academias del asesinato
¡El aliento de la Revolución!"

La Muerte de Práxedis G. Guerrero

Un tiro repentino
En el rojo amanecer
Que no ve la bala ciega
La yegua que se encabrita y se desboca
Se cae de la silla
¡El sollozo de Las Adelitas!

Los Huesos de Práxedis G. Guerrero

Un busto de bronce
Pagado por el estado que él tanto odiaba
En un cementerio polvoroso
De Janos Chihuahua
Calaveras de dulce azúcar
Una calaca sonriente
Danza desenfrenadamente
En la noche de los Muertos.

¡Que muera el Mal Gobierno!
¡Que viva Práxedis G. Guerrero!
¡Que viva la Revolución Mexicana!

- John Ross, 1938-2011

Traducción e Ilustración por Lester Doré   ●   Impresión y Tipografía por Gabriel Quintas C.
Oaxaca de Juárez, Oaxaca   —   Linotipográfica Quintas

La Vida Heroica de Práxedis G. Guerrero, 2011, broadside printed on white commercial paper 43 x 35 cm. Poem by John Ross, engraving on HDPE by Lester Doré, typography by Gabriel Quintas. The Spanish version of the Guerrero broadside was translated by Lester Doré, with help from friends, and published in Oaxaca, Mexico, in October, 2011. The type was hand set by Gabriel Quintas and printed on his vintage Chandler & Price platen press at his shop, Linotipográfica Quintas. About 50 were printed on a commercial text paper and another 100 on "*papel revolucionario*" (newsprint). Most of them were given to celebrants crowding the Zócalo on El Día de los Muertos.

JOHN ROSS

Poet • Journalist • Raconteur • Globetrotting Troublemaker

MADISON STOPS ON HIS NATIONWIDE TOUR

SUNDAY MARCH 14 : 7-9PM
"Iraqigirl", the diary of a teenager growing up under U.S. Occupation
Booktalk with John Ross and Elizabeth Wrigley-Field at
The Dardanelles Restaurant, 1851 Monroe Street.
Co-sponsored by Madison-Rafah Sister-City Project and Haymarket Books

MONDAY MARCH 15: NOON-1PM
A Public Affair, a call-in show with host Norman Stockwell
on WORT-89.9FM

WEDNESDAY MARCH 17: 7-9 PM
"El Monstruo - Historias de la Ciudad de Mexico" Community event with
Spanish-speaking workers at Centro Hispano. (*Event will be in Spanish*)
Centro Hispano, 810 W. Badger Road
Co-Sponsors: Community Action on Latin America and Centro Hispano.

THURSDAY MARCH 18: NOON-1PM
"1810-1910-2010: Will The Mexican Revolution Come Again?"
Brownbag at UW-LACIS, 336 Ingraham Hall

THURSDAY MARCH 18: 7 PM
"El Monstruo - Dread & Redemption in Mexico City" Booksigning
Rainbow Bookstore 426 W. Gilman St.

John Ross's visit to Madison is funded in part by UW-LACIS; A.E. Havens Center; CALA, MATC-Madison, and Edgewood College.

Poster, 28 x 43 cm, designed by Lester Doré for John Ross's visit to Madison in March 2010. Original engraving on HDPE by Lester Doré, printed at Lakeside Press, Madison, Wisconsin, autographed by John Ross. Ross was on a tour promoting his last book, *El Monstruo*, his picaresque history of México City and *IraqiGirl*, a collection of writings by a teenage blogger living in Mosul during the U.S. invasion and occupation of Iraq, edited by Ross and Elizabeth Wrigley-Field.

John Ross signing prints at the home of artist Lester Doré, March 2010. Photo by Norman Stockwell.

John Ross signing prints at the home of artist Lester Doré, March 2010. Photo by Norman Stockwell.

Brad Will, October 25, 2006, in Oaxaca, two days before his death. Photo: Indy-Media.

This altar, with Brad Will's photo in the center, was part of a show of altars and art at the Escape Java Joint and Gallery on Williamson Street in Madison, Wisconsin, in November 2008. The show was organized by activists, artists, and community members for the celebration of El Dia de los Muertos. Brad's parents were present for a talk by Gustavo Vilchis, a *compañero* of Brad's, on his then just published book, *Teaching Rebellion*. Photo by Lester Doré.

Part II

Who Killed Brad Will?

Who Killed Brad Will?

This story was originally commissioned by the Association of Alternative Newsweeklies and edited by the San Francisco Bay Guardian.

"We are an army of dreamers and therefore invincible."
—Subcomandante Marcos[1]
(codicil to Brad Will's final e-mails)

THE LISTS

The New York-based Indymedia gadfly Brad Will caught two 9mm slugs on the barricades in Oaxaca, Mexico, during a furious face-off with the pistoleros of a despised governor on October 27, 2006. He became the newest victim in a continuum of U.S. reporters who have traveled to Mexico to document the struggle for justice, and perhaps assuage their personal demons, often winding up in a shallow grave or on the receiving end of an assassin's bullet, under enigmatic circumstances.

One of the first was Ambrose Bierce, author of *The Devil's Dictionary*, who came to Mexico on assignment for the Hearst papers in 1913 to ride with Pancho Villa and cover his revolution. "The Old Gringo," as Carlos Fuentes dubbed him in the novel of the same name, disappeared at the Battle of Ojinaga and his bones long ago blew to dust out there in the northern desert.

Phillip True, an adventuresome sort stringing for the *San Antonio Express-News* who wandered into the wrong dope patch while on a walkabout in Huichol Indian country in 1998 and never filed another story, was the last U.S. reporter to bite the dust in Mexico before Brad Will caught the bullet that had always borne his name.

71

Brad Will made other lists too. He was one of 26 souls to die on the barricades of Oaxaca from May 2006 to January 2007, and the ninth reporter working in Mexico to have been killed or disappeared during 2006, most under the guns of the narco gangs. Since 2000, 21 have been slain.

Reporters Without Borders lists 85 confirmed kills of journalists during 2006 with whom Brad shares that dubious distinction. Thirty-two media workers also went down in that same time frame. These totals represent a 20% increase over 2005 and are the highest since 1994 when revolutions were roaring in Sri Lanka and Algeria. With Iraq setting the pace, taking out the messenger has become de rigueur. All of us who work the front lines of social upheaval in this corner of the Americas intuit that we could wind up on these lists any day of the week. There is always a bullet out there with our name written on it if we do our work diligently enough.

EL NORTE

Brad Will came from a long way off to find his bullet. We drive along the North Shore out of Chicago through Evanston and Winnetka, Kenilworth and Glencoe, towns where the robber barons who kept what was then the industrial heartland of North America in thrall—George Pullman, Cyrus McCormick, Charles Walgreen—built their mansions and maintained their palatial estates. Now the clipped hedges and billiard table lawns are tended by Mexicans, some of them just in from Oaxaca.

Born in 1970, the year of Cambodia and Kent State, and the youngest of four siblings, Brad grew up across the tracks—the commuter tracks—in Kenilworth, one of the wealthiest enclaves in the nation. Back in 1893 when the town was first developed, the real estate moguls ballyhooed it as "the city of the future" where every home would have maximum sunlight and lake breezes in the summertime. Residents, all of whom were white and Christian, would be swaddled by lush golf courses and ample green spaces, the schools would be superior.

But by the middle of the 20th century, people who actually worked for a living began moving into Kenilworth. Ken Duffy, a neighbor of the Willses, came up on the south side of Chicago where every head of family was either a steelworker or a cop. "I'm probably the only White Sox fan in this town," he jokes as he walks me across Brier Street to the brick colonial where the Will brood was raised and young Brad once sleepwalked out of a second-story window. "He didn't even get scratched. That kid lived a charmed life—until this thing happened," Ken reflects.

Brad Will's violent demise in Mexico still casts a pall over this quiet tree-lined street. "That boy was a dreamer," Ken's wife Betty, a schoolteacher, muses as she fingers an "Action People" television truck that once belonged to Brad—his initials are inked on the toy's chassis so that her kids and the Will gang wouldn't get them mixed up when they played in each other's houses. Betty knew young Brad "from kindergarten to the Boy Scouts" and his sad, sudden death shook her. "He was different from the other boys. At the Little League games, all the kids would be running around and yelling and Brad would just sit there, looking up at the clouds...."

New Trier, one of the nation's top-ranked public high schools, was just five blocks northeast of Brier Street across the Winnetka township line. Among the school's elite alumni are Donald Rumsfeld and Charlton Heston, Charles Percy and Rock Hudson. On an early spring morning, the streets around New Trier are dense with SUVs as athletic-looking, mostly blond boys in shorts warm up for lacrosse practice.

The ambience exudes privilege, but for art historian Melanie Herzog, New Trier was an ordeal. Drug use and classmate suicides were a regular feature of school life: "The pressure to get into an Ivy League school was incredible." Once a friend invited her to sleep over—"she told me I would be the first Jew to ever stay at her house." Although restrictive covenants were abolished by the U.S. Supreme Court in 1948, Kenilworth remains a largely white, gentile community.

Brad was not on the Ivy League track at New Trier.

Julie Johnson, who has taught English literature to nearly two generations of New Trier students, turned Brad on to Thoreau's *Walden* and Conrad's *Heart of Darkness*. She too was stunned by his murder. "The Brad I knew always sought a peaceful resolution when there were conflicts. He was altruistic and not just out for himself as so many kids are these days."

Among Brad's contemporaries at New Trier were the playwright Sarah Ruhl and best-selling author Rich Cohen. "Brad was an extraordinary writer and an extraordinary young man. Anyone who was capable of killing him must be a lunatic," Ruhl told me during a recent telephone interview.

Brad Will broke out of the comfortable bubble of Brier Street in 1988 and headed off to Allegheny, a small liberal arts college near Pittsburgh that describes itself on its web page as being "wonderfully weird." Four years later, he took a sheepskin in English literature. The Beat Generation revival was flourishing by the early 1990s and the adventurous Will hit the road for the Jack Kerouac School of Disembodied Poetics in Boulder, Colorado.

"Basically, we just squatted Naropa. We went to all the classes, but we were never enrolled. Anne Waldman really got on our case," remembers Jenny Smith, a tired-eyed poet with blazing red hair during an ad hoc post-mortem at Bluestockings bookstore on the Lower East Side of Manhattan. Smith was Will's on-and-off lover for 12 years.

Brad's guru at Naropa was Peter Lamborn Wilson, aka Hakim Bey,[2] whose visionary gravitational pull soon ensnared the young man. Bey, whose text *Temporary Autonomous Zones, Ontological Anarchy, and Poetic Trea-*

son has had resonance with a new generation of anarchists, once presided at Brad's wedding (Brad was in drag) to another man during a Promise Keepers séance in Boulder to protest Colorado's draconian anti-gay laws. This was, perhaps, the late activist-journalist's first act of public defiance.

Under Bey's tutelage, Brad moved into Dreamtime Village, a cutting-edge community in southern Wisconsin where he perused the mysteries of hypermedia and permaculture, and where Bey, the godfather of the Rave movement, spoke of building "pirate utopias."

The next pit stop on this restless odyssey that would eventually lead Brad Will to a bullet on the barricades of Oaxaca, Mexico, was New York City's Lower East Side where he touched down in the company of the comic artist Fly in late 1994. "It was a hard time for the financially disinclined," Will recalled in a narrative published after his death in *The Indypendent*, an Indymedia newspaper. Giuliani had just been elected mayor and the developers were running amuck in the neighborhood, bulldozing building after building to make way for the condo crowd. Brad and a band of crazies moved into a crumbling tenement on Fifth Street in Alphabet City and resuscitated the building—only to have it ripped out from under them after a fire, purportedly triggered when Will kicked over his space heater, gave the city a pretext to deconstruct the edifice. The grainy Paper Tiger TV footage of Brad up on the roof, flapping his long arms like Big Bird as the wrecking ball swung in, made this young son of privilege a living legend—at least down on the Lower East Side.

The 1994 Zapatista rebellion in Chiapas had caught Brad's attention. The Mayan rebels' demand for autonomy in Chiapas dovetailed into the space Bey had brought him to—of which the community gardens movement in New York was another expression. Saving the Chico Mendes Mural Garden on Avenue B became an obsession—it was ploughed under by the city in 1998. The More Gardens Coalition turned its energies to the defense of the Esperanza Garden on Seventh Street where Brad led the lockdown when the cops came for it. Giuliani's grab to annihilate 119 gardens met with a lively sit-in under the rotunda at City Hall—Will was dragged off dressed as a sunflower. La Esperanza was demolished but all the other gardens on Giuliani's hit list received court protection and are growing still.

Brad Will honed his skills in non-violent resistance at Ruckus camps[3] out in the woods on both coasts, learning how to climb smokestacks and "monkeywrench"[4] the American Way of Life. He rode freight trains out west and barges down the Mississippi. He sat in old-growth Douglas firs up at the Fall Creek Earth First! action outside of Eugene, Oregon. He was friends until the end with Daniel McGowan, the accused eco-terrorist, and Free (Jeffrey Luers), who is now pulling 20 years for torching a car lot full of SUVs.

Brad was busted in Seattle during the landmark 1999 demonstration against the World Trade Organization. Indymedia was born from the loins of the Nation of Seattle and Brad was an early enabler. Will caught the anti-globalization bug and fanned out to protests in Prague and Quebec City and Genoa—he once boasted that he had been in four riots in six countries during a six-month-long European sojourn in 2000.

Brad was everywhere in New York during those incandescent years. He rode with Critical Mass, and the tale of Will picking up his bike and running over the tops of four cars in Times Square to escape New York's Finest has secured him a spot in the pantheon of the city's street heroes.

Brad Will had a weekly show on Steal This Radio, the pirate station on the Lower East Side whose studios one accessed by climbing a ladder lowered from a second-story window. He was a Food-Not-Bomber[5] and a dumpster diver—he favored the ones behind health food stores because he liked to eat well. His method of eating free at salad bars was exemplary. "He was a sincere mooch," laughs Rob Jereski, a fellow gardener. Brad was a true believer in "Freeganism" and did his damnedest to live outside of the money economy. With his long hair tied neatly in back and parted down the middle, his scruffy beard and granny glasses and fierce determination to build community, Brad Will seemed indeed a persona from a more Utopian past.

Brad Will was also a musician who brought spirit to hundreds of community gatherings. He lived his music and was, says Jenny, a rather reckless dancer. He was literally a fire-breather, breathing flames at public protests to the consternation of Giuliani's police. By 2004, ABC News was claiming Brad Will to be one of America's 50 most dangerous anarchists[6] and the cops had him redlined at the Republican National Convention.

But the fiery socio-cultural stew that found a home on the Lower East Side was extinguished by another fire just a few blocks south on September 11, 2001. Nine-eleven put a damper on the resistance movement and the spark began to sputter.

Dyan Neary, then a neophyte journalist, met Brad in the elevator coming down from the WBAI studios in the South Street skyscraper where Amy Goodman used to broadcast, until she moved into the old Chinatown fire station. "We walked down to the piles. They were still smoking," she remembered in a phone call from Humboldt County, California. "We were both really scared. We thought this was not going to be resolved soon. Maybe never. So we thought we should go to Latin America where people were still fighting back."

HEADING SOUTH

"I suppose Brad started going south because that's where he saw the hope was," figured Mark Read, a co-conspirator, during the Bluestockings huddle. "The people filled Brad with spirit," Dyan adds. "We thought we could go down there and bring back their stories and that would get the movement going again."

In January 2002, four months after 9/11, Brad and Dyan fought Giuliani's jittery police at the World Economic Forum, an annual get-together of the most powerful business interests on the planet that had moved its yearly conclave from an ice mountain in Switzerland to New York in solidarity with the damaged city. The Big Apple was still in shock and the streets were not filled with angry throngs. It was freezing. Brad got arrested anyway—Dyan thought it was his twentieth bust. They flew to Ecuador soon after.

Brad and Dyan spent most of 2002 and 2003 roaming the bubbling social landscape of Latin America. In Fortaleza, Brazil, they confronted Enrique Iglesias, the director of the InterAmerican Development Bank, during riotous street protests. They celebrated the "Argentinazo," the economic meltdown that stirred popular rebellion in Buenos Aires and crashed with the *piquete-ros* (unemployed) and the *escraches* who harassed those responsible for the dirty war that disappeared 30,000 leftists in the late 1970s. It was a circuit followed by a lot of anti-globalization, pro-Zapatista anarchists in those first heady years of the pendulum swing to the left that had the continent thrumming with possibility—and hope.

Brad and Dyan journeyed to Bolivia, too, and interviewed Evo Morales, not yet the president, and traveled in the Chapare with the coca-growers' federation. They hung out in Cochabamba with Oscar Olivera, the hero of the battle to keep Bechtel from taking over the city's water system. Everywhere they went, they sought out pirate radio projects and offered their solidarity.

"When we came back to New York in late 2003, we did talks and presentations to raise money for these projects and to go back again," Dyan continues. While they were down south, Bush had launched his genocidal war in Iraq, and the anti-war movement had revived street mobilizations. The battle royal at the 2004 Republican Convention was a high point but Bush's re-election in November definitely was not. The movement slunk back into paralysis.

Brad seemed more serious after his travels, thought Brandon Jourdan, an affable Indymedia cameraperson who had been beaten to a pulp with Will at the 2003 Miami FTAA Summit of the Americas for trying to film John Timoney's police riot. For a while Brandon and Brad shared live-work space with Big Noise films (Rick Rowley and Jacquie Soohen) near Canal Street. Brad had decided to dedicate himself to documenting peoples' struggles and was working now and then as a stagehand and sound techie, stashing his bucks to head south again. Where the hope was.

In February 2005 Brad was back on the ground in Brazil in the thick of social upheaval, filming the resistance of 12,000 squatters at a camp near the city of Goiana in Pernambuco state when the military police swept in, killing two and disappearing and jailing hundreds. You can hear the live ammunition zinging all around him as he captures the carnage—the bullet with his name on it had come a lot closer that day. Will was savagely beaten and held by the police. Only his U.S. passport saved him.

Brad thought about Goiana while recuperating on the edge of São Paolo. In an e-mail to Dyan, he wrote that he was haunted by one of the disappeared. He kept seeing his face. "For a long time, it has been in my bones." Will was also not much impressed by the new leaders of the Latin left—the repression at Goiana came down under socialist President Luiz Inácio "Lula" da Silva.

Undaunted by his close call, Brad Will picked up his camera and soldiered back through Peru and Bolivia and when the money ran out, flew back to New York to figure out how to raise enough scratch for the next trip south. He was hooked.

In early 2006, like a moth to the flame, he was back, tracking Subcomandante Marcos and the Zapatistas' Other Campaign through the Mayan villages on Mexico's Yucatán peninsula. From the Yucatán, it was just a short hop across the Caribbean to Caracas for Hugo Chávez's World Social Forum. Not content to hobnob with the lefty mob and cheer on Comandante Chávez, Brad ventured into Indian territory to film resistance to a government dam. He had learned a valuable lesson from Lula's police at Goiana: it was the people and not the leaders whose story he was committed to telling.

Brad's ear was glued to Mexico in the spring of 2006 as he tracked the Other Campaign on the Internet from his room in Williamsburg across the river in Brooklyn—the rent gougers had forced him off the Lower East Side at last. The brutal repression on May 3 and 4 at San Salvador Atenco, when the cops killed two young men and raped women protesters soon after the Other Campaign had visited the town, almost had Brad flying south that night. Brad and Brandon marched outside the Mexican Consulate on Park Avenue and 39th Street in June following similar repression in Oaxaca.

Despite working 60-hour weeks, Will showed up at protests when he could. That summer, Tim Keating met up with Brad at an action outside a Victoria's Secret store to save old-growth forests—the lingerie titan prints 400,000,000 catalogues. They were about to release 40 helium balloons when the cops spotted them and confiscated the offending props. Just days before he flew off to Oaxaca, he was back at the Mexican consulate for a protest.

Brandon thought his friend was spreading himself too thin: "He was like one of these old buildings with all the faucets turned on—there wasn't much water pressure."

Brad was following the uprising in Oaxaca on Radio Universidad, the voice of the rebellion. He was poised to jump south but worried that he would just be one more white guy getting in the way. He would have to give up a lot of work to film the struggle, but in the end the lure of the Commune of Oaxaca pulled him in. He wrote Al Giordano, the big daddy of *Narco News*, one of the better sources for what was coming down on the ground, but Giordano cautioned him against going to Oaxaca. *Narco News* insiders say Giordano thought Brad too reckless, a loose cannon.

Will was stung by the rebuff but bought a 30-day ticket anyway. He caught the airport shuttle from Brooklyn to JFK and flew south September 29, 2007. His return was set for October 28. He never made the plane.

THE COMMUNE OF OAXACA

Oaxaca had been laying for Brad Will for a long time, millennia maybe. A mountainous southern Mexican state traversed by seven serious sierras, Oaxaca is up at the top of most poverty indicators—infant mortality, malnutrition, unemployment, and illiteracy. Human rights violations are rife. Coincidentally, Oaxaca is Mexico's most indigenous state, with 17 distinct Indian cultures, each with a rich tradition of resistance to the dominant white and mestizo overclass. Oaxaca vibrates with class and race tensions that cyclically erupt into uprising and repression.

In 1987, I came to Oaxaca to investigate the massacre of 26 Indian farmers in the district of Sola de Vega. The dispute that led to the killings centered on forestry rights in the southern Zapotec sierra. Men from Amoltepec led by a thug named Antonio Roque had ambushed a group of campesinos from Santa María Zanisa. No one was talking by the time I got there. Fifteen years later, on April 11, 2002, another massacre took place in the same district, again over forestry rights granted both Amoltepec and Zanisa by the government. This time the toll was 28. Antonio Roque, who had served ten years in prison for his part in the previous massacre, was now the PRI municipal president of Amoltepec. Politics and injustice are intrinsically entwined in Oaxaca.

The Party of the Institutional Revolution or PRI ruled Mexico from 1928 through 2000, the longest-running political dynasty in the known universe until it was beaten at the polls in July 2000 by the right-wing National Action Party (PAN) and its picaresque presidential candidate Vicente Fox, former president of Coca-Cola Mexico.

But in Oaxaca, the PRI never lost power. While all over the country voters were throwing off the PRI yoke, in Oaxaca one PRI governor had followed another for 75 years when Ulises Ruiz Ortiz (called "URO"), a protégé of party strongman and future presidential candidate Roberto Madrazo, stole the gubernatorial elections from a right-left coalition in 2004.

Although Gabino Cué had apparently won the election, the PRI's classic *modus operandi* snatched it away from him. A rash of stolen ballot boxes and myriad irregularities in the polling places and the vote count (the PRI controlled the electoral machinery) awarded the vote to URO by a minimal margin—the vote-tallying computers crashed three times on election night. When Cué led protests against the flimflam, Ruiz threatened to toss him in jail.

Ulises's inauguration January 15, 2005, was a tableau of how he intended to govern Oaxaca. Thousands of state and municipal police cordoned off the stately plaza of that old colonial capital to crush any signal of dissonance. Ruiz would rule with a hard hand (*mano dura*)—30 social activists suffered violent deaths in the first two years of his governance and dozens more were imprisoned. In August 2005, Ulises greenlighted goons from a spurious PRI union to lay siege to the offices of the opposition daily *Noticias*—the paper's editorial staff was held hostage for nearly a hundred days.

"All that Oaxaqueños really want are *chapulines* [roasted grasshoppers, a local delicacy] and *tasajo* [grilled steak]," the new governor told *Proceso* magazine soon after his inauguration, a Oaxacan version of Marie Antoinette's "let them eat cake" philosophy. Ruiz promptly moved all government offices out of the center of the capital to a distant suburb, where he would be insulated from demonstrations, but miscalculated badly when he tried to dismantle the city's beloved town square under the masquerade of "modernization," and what remained of his popularity plummeted to a new low.

In the first 16 months of his regime, Ulises Ruiz had proven spectacularly unresponsive to the demands of the popular movements for social justice. When on May 15, 2006, National Teachers' Day, Section 22, a maverick, militant local of the National Education Workers Union (SNTE), presented its contract demands, Ruiz turned a deaf ear. Then on May 22, as Section 22 had done every year since its founding in 1979, tens of thousands of teachers took the plaza and 52 surrounding blocks and set up a ragtag tent city. Each morning, the *maestros* would march out of their camp and block highways and government buildings, which were soon smeared with anti-URO slogans.

Ruiz retaliated before dawn on June 14, sending a thousand heavily armed police into the plaza to evict the teachers. Low-flying helicopters sprayed pepper gas on the throng below. Ruiz's police had taken up positions in the colonial hotels that surround the plaza and smashed down concussion grenades from the balconies. Radio Plantón, the *maestros'* pirate radio station, was demolished and the tent city set afire. A pall of black smoke hung over the city. Nonetheless, URO called a press conference to insist there had been no confrontation.

Four hours later, a spontaneous outburst from Oaxaca's very active civil society and the force of the striking teachers, armed with clubs and Molotov cocktails, overran the plaza and sent URO's cops packing. No uniformed police officers would be seen on the streets of Oaxaca for many months. And on June 16, two days after the monumental battle, 200,000 Oaxacans marched through the city to repudiate the governor's "hard hand." The mega march was said to extend ten kilometers.

John Gibler, who closely covered the Oaxaca uprising as a human rights fellow for Global Exchange, writes that the surge of the civil society June 14 soon transformed itself into a popular assembly.[7] The Oaxaca People's Popular Assembly or APPO was formally constituted a week later on June 21. The APPO would have no leaders but many spokespersons, and all decisions had to be taken in popular assemblies.

For the next weeks, the APPO and Section 22 would paralyze Oaxaca but the rest of Mexico took little notice. Instead, the nation was hypnotized by the fraud-marred July 2 presidential election in which a right-wing PANista, Felipe Calderón, had been awarded a narrow victory over leftist Andrés Manuel López Obrador (AMLO), the candidate of a coalition headed by the Party of the Democratic Revolution (PRD.) López Obrador was quick to cry fraud, pulling millions into the streets, the most massive political demonstrations in Mexican history.[8] Oaxaca still seemed like small potatoes.

Ulises Ruiz had pledged a million votes to his patron Madrazo, who finished a dismal third in the balloting. But as if July 2 had been a referendum on URO's fortunes, the Oaxaca electorate applied *el voto de castigo* (a punishment vote) and AMLO walked off with the state plus a bonus gift for his PRD of two senators and nine out of 11 congressional representatives, the first time ever the PRI had lost Oaxaca. Ulises suddenly dropped out of public view.

Oaxaca is an international tourist destination—state and city economic life is tourist-driven. But now the APPO and Section 22 had closed down the tourist infrastructure, blocking the airport and forcing five-star hotels to shutter their doors. On July 17, still hiding out (probably at the Laureles Hotel in a wealthy neighborhood of the city), Ruiz announced the cancellation of the *Guelaguetza*, an "indigenous" dance festival that has become Oaxaca's premiere tourist attraction, after roaming bands of rebels destroyed the scenery and blockaded access to the city. Later, the APPO and Section 22 would stage a "popular" *Guelaguetza* with its roots in *intercambio* between Oaxaca's distinct and idiosyncratic indigenous cultures, in the part of the city they continued to occupy.

By the end of July, frustrated by the inattention of the federal government and congress to remove URO—the country was still embroiled in post-electoral turmoil—the APPO voted to up the ante and make Oaxaca ungovernable.

On the day after Ulises's goons had taken down Radio Plantón, June 15, student supporters of the striking teachers seized the Benito Juárez Autonomous University campus radio station and Radio Universidad became the voice of the rebellion. *Doctora Escopeta* (Doctor Shotgun), a husky-voiced professor named Berta Muñoz, stayed on the air 24-7 offering logistical support and spurring on the struggle as troubadours strummed stirring songs of social change. Brad Will, himself a pirate radio star on "Steal This Radio," was listening in Brooklyn.

The battle for control of the airwaves got very physical very quickly.[9] At the end of July, gunmen opened fire on Radio Universidad, knocking it off the air temporarily. In response, thousands of APPO and Section 22 supporters led by women activists invaded CORTV-Channel 9, Ulises's statewide TV mouthpiece, and held it for weeks despite nightly drive-by shootings by the governor's goons, mostly off-duty cops.

When, finally, the gunmen were able to take out the transmitter, the rebels marched on 12 commercial stations and occupied them. Ulises's pistoleros concentrated their fire on *La Ley* (The Law) radio, where a major gun battle erupted on August 21.

The governor's gunmen were drawn from the ranks of the city police force and the state ministerial cops. Security agents busied themselves infiltrating APPO and teachers' meetings. One such undercover operator was captured and stripped naked by an APPO mob.

The absence of street enforcement reportedly had brought a pilgrimage of *rateros* (thieves) to town, and impromptu neighborhood watch groups responded with vigilante tactics, pummeling suspects and lashing them to lampposts with signs around their necks advertising that they were *rateros*. In this hothouse atmosphere, the press was not above suspicion. Gibler reports that a colleague with close ties to the cops was set upon and beaten so badly he had to be hospitalized.

By the first weeks in August, URO launched what came to be known as his "Caravan of Death"—a train of 30 to 40 private and government vehicles—rolling nightly, firing on the protesters. José Luis Colmenares, the husband of a striking teacher, was gunned down by Ulises's sharpshooters during a march of 20,000 through the city on August 10. A mass funeral was held before thousands in the seething plaza. On August 22, architect Lorenzo San Pablo, an APPO supporter, was cut down while talking with a neighbor near the center of the city.

To keep the Caravans of Death from moving freely through the city, the APPO and the *maestros* threw up barricades—a thousand were built in the working-class colonies throughout the city and its suburbs. The rebels piled up dead trees, old tires, the carcasses of burnt-out cars and buses to build the barricades, which soon took on a life of their own—murals were painted with the ashes of the bonfires that burnt all night on the barriers. It was indeed the barricades that gave the Oaxaca struggle the romantic aura of the Paris Commune and attracted droves of dreadlocked anarchists to the city.

Late in August Televisa, the nation's top TV octopus, aired some instructive footage shot by its Oaxaca correspondent Iván Soldaña, on its primetime nightly news. Soldaña and a cameraperson had joined the Caravan of

Death in an unmarked car and driven around the city with the gun thugs in the early morning dark, surreptitiously filming as the gunmen fired at the barricades, then trailing them back to a police barracks where the cops called it a night.

Despite the visual evidence of URO's complicity in perpetrating the violence, President Fox made no move to replace Ulises with a less homicidal governor. His hands were tied until the presidential election shook down.[10]

Charges that guerrilla organizations had infiltrated the APPO and the teachers' movement were frequently leveled by Ulises's underlings. Secretary of Government Heliodoro Díaz accused Section 22 President Enrique Rueda Pacheco of being an operative of the Popular Revolutionary Army (EPR), a nearly dormant guerrilla band. Ruiz's drop-dead gorgeous state prosecutor Lizbeth Caña Cadeza denounced the APPO as "a subversive urban guerrilla," an unproven accusation much quoted by AP stringer Rebeca Romero, who was fired in 2007 by the news service for being on URO's payroll.

As if scripted, ski-masked "guerrillas" passed out leaflets at crossroads outside the capital and the EPR's initials magically appeared painted in huge letters on a hill overlooking the city. The War On Terror had come to Oaxaca. On August 24, U.S. Ambassador Tony Garza issued an urgent travel advisory warning *gringos* to stay away from the state.

A flurry of negotiations that went nowhere took place in September. The APPO met with Fox's interior minister, Carlos Abascal, as did representatives of Section 22, but their only demand now was the removal of Ulises Ruiz Ortiz as governor of the state. Politically, Fox's PAN could not do that lest it drive off the PRI whose votes in the lower house of the new congress the PAN desperately needed.

While negotiations sputtered along in Mexico City, down on the ground in Oaxaca painter Francisco Toledo, a hometown hero who had once kept a McDonald's from setting up in the plaza, sought to work out an acceptable truce, but his home was shot up and he turned over the job to aging Chiapas bishop emeritus Samuel Ruiz who had once worked out a shaky peace agreement between the Zapatistas and the government. Don Samuel, too, retired in frustration.

An uneasy lull in the action gripped Oaxaca when Brad Will arrived at the ADO bus terminal on October 1 and found himself a cheap room for the night. The break in the action wouldn't last long. The bullet with Brad's name on it was already locked into the chamber.

DEATH ON THE BARRICADES

John Gibler, who had been covering the conflict since July and often reported for *Democracy Now!*, ran into Brad on Will's second day in town. He remembered the lanky, ginger-bearded Indymedia photojournalist from Chetumal back in January when they were both on the road with Subcomandante Marcos and the Zapatistas' Other Campaign as it wended its way through the Yucatán peninsula. Brad had been kissed off by *Narco News* and needed contacts badly. They went off for coffee and Gibler gave the newcomer a crash course on who to see and how to watch his back. Hang with the national and the local press, John encouraged, they know the ropes. "Brad was a smart guy," Gibler recalled over lunch in Mexico City, "but how smart can you be when the cops shoot you in the heart?"

Over the next days, Brad Will took time to figure out where he was. His Spanish wasn't very good and it bugged him. He found a place to crash, a squat with other "internationals" that was rumored to once have been a police station. Eating was a hassle. Brad had come to Mexico eating only raw, uncooked foods. "It gives you a buzz like cocaine but without the crash," he wrote Dyan. But eating raw in Mexico invites Montezuma's Revenge, so he got by on beans and rice.

Brad made the rounds of the NGOs and human rights organizations, established contact with Section 22 and the APPO and hung out at the Council of Indigenous People of Oaxaca or CIPO-RFM (the last three letters are the initials of Oaxaca-born anarchist Ricardo Flores Magón, a seminal figure in the Mexican revolution). He started walking the barricades every day, giving himself plenty of time to do interviews with the militants. He was determined to bring their stories back with him so that U.S. activists could draw energy from the Commune of Oaxaca.

Like most non-Mexican activists who style themselves as independent reporters, Brad Will had no Mexican press credential and therefore was in the country illegally, working on a tourist visa and susceptible to deportation under Article 33 of the Mexican constitution, which gives the president carte blanche to throw any *extranjero* (literally "stranger" but the everyday term for non-Mexican) out of the country if he or she was deemed "inconvenient" to the country's interests. Article 33 was a favorite mechanism for deporting over 400 "inconvenient" *extranjeros* from Chiapas at the height of the Zapatista rebellion.

So that he would have some credential other than his Indymedia press card to hang around his neck, Brad got himself accredited at Section 22 and wore the ID assiduously. It demonstrated that he was not with the *prensa vendida*—the press that was for sale—and stood with the people of Oaxaca.

By the second week of October, the lull had definitely snapped. Apparently encouraged by the national exposure they had received on Televisa,

Ulises's death squads continued to roll every night and on October 14, APPO militant Alejandro García Hernández was cut down at a barricade near the corner of *Símbolos Patrios* (Patriotic Symbols) downtown. Brad joined an angry procession to the Red Cross hospital where the dead man had been taken. On the way, he noticed a wall that had been riddled with bullets by Ulises's killers and thought about Amadou Diallo, the African street vendor cruelly executed by Giuliani's cops.

Brad admitted to Dyan that he was not prepared for what he encountered at the morgue—"I haven't seen many dead bodies before." There was no refrigeration and the taste of putrefaction was on his tongue. The dead man was laid out on his slab, his skull cut away by the coroner, Dr. Luis Mendoza, to extract the bullet. His family surrounded him, quietly weeping. The photographers' flashbulbs popped off like small arms fire. Pop! Pop! Pop!

On October 16 in the last dispatch that he filed from Oaxaca, Brad Will caught this very Mexican whiff of death. "Now [Alejandro] lies there waiting for November 2, the Day of the Dead, when he can sit with his loved ones again to share food and drink and song....

"One more death. One more time to cry and hurt. One more time to know power and its ugly head. One more bullet cracks the night."

One of those bullets had Brad's name inscribed upon it. Now that he had come to Oaxaca, it was looking for him.

"I went back to the morgue," Brad wrote Dyan on October 24. "It is a sick and sad place. I have a feeling I will go back there again with a crowd of reporters all pushing to get the money shot."

The dynamic in Oaxaca had gotten "sketchy" was how he described it to Dyan. Section 22 leader Rueda Pacheco had cut a deal with the outgoing Fox government and forced a back-to-work vote October 21 that narrowly carried amidst charges of sell-out and pay-offs. If the teachers went back to work, the APPO would be alone on the barricades and even more vulnerable to Ulises's gun thugs. But backing down is not in the Popular Assembly's dictionary and the APPO voted to ratchet up the *lucha* (struggle) and make Oaxaca really ungovernable.

Mobile brigades were formed, *turbas* (gangs) of young toughs armed with lead pipes and boards with nails driven through them who hijacked what buses were still running in the city, forced the passengers off, and rode around looking for action. Later, the buses would be set afire. Charred hulks blossomed on the streets of the old colonial city. The barricades were reinforced to shut down the capital beginning October 27.

The escalation proved to be a terrible miscalculation. Up in Mexico City, the post-electoral turmoil had finally subsided and the PAN was ready to deal with the PRI—bailing out Ulises was the price of admission. By torqueing up the troubles in Oaxaca, the APPO had gifted Fox with a golden opportunity to send in the troops.

The xenophobia had become palpable in the city. Ulises's people were checking the guest lists at the hostels for "inconvenient" internationals. Immigration authorities threatened *extranjeros* with Article 33 if they joined the protests. The local U.S. consul, Mark Leyes, warned Americans that he would not be able to help them out if they got caught up in the maelstrom.

To add to this malevolent ambience, a new pirate radio station popped up at 99 on the FM dial October 26. Radio Ciudadana (Citizens' Radio) was broadcasting "to bring peace to Oaxaca" and to celebrate the honor of "our macho, very macho governor." CIPO's Miguel Cruz, who tuned in on the barricades thinks the transmitter was located at the Laureles Hotel where URO was holed up. Others suggest it was a mobile unit.

The announcers seemed to have Chilango (Mexico City) accents. Wherever they had been sent from, they let loose with a torrent of vitriolic sh*t—stuff like "We have to kill the *mugrosos* (dirty ones) on the barricades." The *extranjeros* were stirring up all the trouble. "They pretend to be journalists but they have come to teach terrorism classes. If one of them is staying in your neighborhood, report him." "*Si ves a un gringo con cámara, ¡mátanlo!*"—literally, "if you see a gringo with a camera, kill him!" This poison spewed out of local radios all day October 26 and 27, but whether Brad heard the warnings and if he did hear them, knew what they meant, is unclear. His Spanish was still not all that great.

Or did he even care? Brad Will had been on the barricades before. The tape of Goiana must have been running in his head. The adrenaline of rebellion is a powerful drug.

Brad called Brandon in New York on the night of the 25—the Indymedia cameraman, who had just gotten back from Lebanon, heard a lot of traffic noise and figured he was calling from the street. Both Brandon and Brad used the same camera—Brad had bought his on eBay and was a little unsure of the settings. He had made contact with Telesur, Hugo Chávez's South American news venture, and they would pay him a pittance for raw footage. Brad wanted to make sure he got it right.

The next day, Brad went out with *compas* from the CIPO to do interviews on the barricade at Santa María Coyotepec, about 20 kilometers from the city. The three barricades at Coyotepec, Cal y Canto, and La Experimental were crucial to closing down Oaxaca on the 27. Brad stayed late and got back to the CIPO compound in Santa Lucía del Camino just outside the city around 10 p.m. "He asked me if he could come by in the morning and edit some film—we have equipment upstairs," Miguel remembers, and then went back to where he was sleeping.

Two would be killed and 13 wounded the next day at Coyotepec—some of them must be on Brad's tape.

Brad showed up early at the CIPO on the 27th. He and Miguel Cruz shared *café* in the compound's open-air kitchen and then he went upstairs to work and Miguel walked out to the barricade at Cal y Canto a few blocks away. Cruz saw Brad again around noon when he stopped by the barricade to chat. The broad Railroad Avenue, where the barricade was built, was empty. Nothing was moving on it. The blockade seemed to be working. Brad walked onto the next barricade at La Experimental to check out the action.

Soon after the Indymedia reporter left, all hell broke loose at Cal y Canto. A mob of about 150 Ulises supporters stormed down Railroad Avenue—they were led by what Cruz thought was a Blazer. The car was moving very fast. "We thought it would try and crash through the barricade." But the SUV stopped short and several men jumped out with guns blazing. The APPO people hunkered down behind the makeshift barrier and moved the women and kids that were with them into a nearby house. Then they went on the counterattack with Molotov cocktails, homemade "bazookas" that fired bottle rockets, slingshots, and perhaps a few small-caliber pistols of their own. Most of the mob had melted away and with the gunmen retreating, the rebels torched their car.

Brad heard about the gunfire while interviewing militants at La Experimental and hurried back to Cal y Canto with a handful of other reporters. They arrived a little after 3 p.m. The gunfire had slowed in the heat of the day. Brad climbs under a parked trailer and shoots the shooters. He focuses in on a man in a white shirt. When an APPO *compa* comes running by (we never see who it is on Brad's last tape) Will indicates the shooter saying "*camisa blanca*." While all this is going on, Brad's camera captures a bicyclist pedaling dreamily through the intersection. Soon after, a large dump truck appears on the scene and the group on the barricade uses it as a mobile shield as they chase the gunmen down the avenue.

Suddenly, the *pistoleros* veer down a narrow side street, Benito Juárez, and take refuge in a windowless one-story building in the second block. The only access to the building is a large metal garage door and the reporters follow the APPO militants, many of them with their faces masked, as they try and force their way in—Brad actually stands to one side of the door for a minute, poised for the "money shot." Then the *compas* try and bust down the big door by ramming the dump truck into it.

In the midst of this frenzy, five men in civilian dress, two in red shirts (Ulises's colors), two in white, and one in a dark blue jacket, appear at the head of Juárez street about 30 meters away. They have run down from the Santa Lucía Municipal Palace just a block west. They are all cops and at least two of them are firing what appear to be .38 Specials. Another is sighting up an M1 rifle.

The two red shirts have been identified as Juan Carlos Martínez Soriano ("*El Chapulín*") and Abel Santiago Zarate ("*El Chino*"). One of the white shirts is Pedro Carmona, a local PRI political fixer and cop. Police Commander Orlando Manuel Aguilar Coello is wearing a blue jacket. Crouched behind him in a white shirt is a local police officer, Juan Sumano. Santiago Zarate and Aguilar Coello are reported to be the personal bodyguards of PRI Municipal President Manuel Martínez Ferrera. All five are eminently identifiable in the film Brad Will and other Mexican news photographers shot before, during, and after his murder by them.

When the shooting erupted, Brad took cover on the opposite side of the narrow street from the rest of the press. He was crouched against a lime green wall when the bullet came for him. You can hear the shot on the sound track and Brad's dismay as it tears through his Indymedia T-shirt and smashes into his chest. A second shot catches him in the right side and destroys his innards. But there is no blood, the first slug having stopped his heart from pumping. On film Gustavo Vilchis and others took, the entrance wound looks like a deep bruise. The second shot is not recorded on the sound track and may have been fired simultaneously with the first one.

Others are hit in the pandemonium. Oswaldo Ramírez, filming for the daily *Milenio*, is grazed in the fusillade. Lucio David Cruz, an unrelated bystander described by Miguel Cruz as being *borracho* (drunk) is shot in the neck and dies four months later.

As Brad slides down the wall into a sitting position, Vilchis and Leonardo Ortiz run to him. His Section 22 credential has flown off and no one really knows his name. With bullets whizzing by, the *compas* pick Brad up—his pants fall off—and drag him out of the line of fire around the corner to Árboles Street about 35 paces away. "Ambulance! We need an ambulance! They've shot a journalist!" Gustavo Vilchis, a tall young man with a face like an Italian comic actor, shouts desperately. Gualberto Francisco has parked his *vochito* (Volkswagen Beetle) on Árboles and pulls up alongside where Brad is laid out on the pavement. slightly elevated, looking suspiciously like a martyred Che,[11] or Jesus Christ, in his black bikini underwear.

Leonardo and Gustavo load a dying Brad Will into the backseat. He is still breathing and Vilchis applies mouth-to-mouth resuscitation. "You're going to make it...you're all right" they keep telling him but Brad's eyes have already receded to the back of his head, *perdido* (lost), as they say here. The *vochito* runs out of gas. "I didn't know I would be using the car for this that day," Gualberto sadly reflects. "We left our *compañero* in the road."

So there they are stuck in the middle of the Cinco Señores crossroad, three frantic young men with a nearly dead gringo reporter and it starts to rain hard. They try and stop a taxi to take them to the Red Cross but the driver supports Ulises and wants to argue. Finally they flag down a pick-up truck and lay Brad out in the bed. He is "Dead On Arrival" by the time the reach the hospital according to Dr. Mendoza's report.

October 27 was the bloodiest day of the Oaxaca uprising. Four others were killed besides Brad and 21 wounded by Ulises's goons. Their names were Emilio Alonso Fabián, Esteban Ruiz, Esteban López Zurita, and Eudocia Olivera Díaz. They should not be forgotten.

Unlike their murders, Brad's death triggered international outrage. Because he was so connected, the shot of the mortally wounded Indymedia reporter lying in the middle of a Oaxaca street went worldwide on the web in a matter of minutes. We had it up on the big screen at New College in San Francisco's Mission District by the time I spoke at 7:30 p.m. that night. There were instant vigils on both coasts. The following Monday, 12 of Brad's friends were busted at the Mexican Consulate off Manhattan's Park Avenue where it still read "Avenge Brad!" and anarchists splattered the San Francisco consulate with red paint. Subcomandante Marcos sent his condolences and called for international protests. Amy Goodman did an hour-long memorial on *Democracy Now!* on Monday morning, October 30.

The official reaction to Brad's death was more cautious. "It is unfortunate when peaceful demonstrations get out of hand and result in violence" a U.S. spokesperson told the press, seeming to blame the APPO for Will's killing. After warning Americans that they traveled to Oaxaca "at their own risk," Ambassador Tony Garza, a Bush crony from his Texas days, commented on the "senseless death of Brad Will" and how it "underscores the need for a return to the rule of law and order. For months, violence and disorder in Oaxaca have worsened. Teachers, students, and other groups have been involved in increasingly violent demonstrations...."

Garza's statement sent President Fox the signal he had been waiting for. Now that a gringo had been killed, it was time to act. The next morning, Saturday, October 28, some 4,500 Federal Preventative Police, an elite force drawn from the military, were sent into Oaxaca not to return the state to a place where human rights and people's dignity and a free press are respected but to break the back of the people's rebellion and maintain Ulises Ruiz Ortiz in power.

The following Sunday the troops pushed their way into the plaza despite massive passive resistance by the civil society, tore down the barricades, and drove the Commune of Oaxaca back into the shadows.

In Mexico, the dead are buried quickly. After Dr. Mendoza had performed the obligatory autopsy, Brad's body was crated up for shipment back to his parents who now live south of Milwaukee. "It took a long time for him to come home," Kathy Will wrote me in an e-mail. The airport was so busy with all the police arriving that Brad was stuck there for several days. He didn't smell very good when he got to Milwaukee. After a private viewing, the family had Brad Will cremated.

THIS IS WHAT IMPUNITY LOOKS LIKE

Killing a gringo reporter here in Mexico in plain view of the cameras (one of which was his own) requires a little sham accountability. On October 29, as the Federal police (PFP) were taking the city, URO's state prosecutor, Lizbeth Caña Cadeza, announced that arrest warrants were being sworn out for *El Chino* (Abel Santiago) and Orlando Manuel Aguilar, two of the five cops pictured gunning Brad Will down, and they were subsequently taken into custody. Two .38 Specials were confiscated—the accused killers had had three days in which to ditch the weapons they had fired on Juárez Street.

This scam lost currency when on November 15th, Lizbeth dropped a bombshell at an evening press conference: Brad Will's death had been "a deceitful confabulation to internationalize the conflict" and was, in fact, "the product of a concerted premeditated action." The mortal shot had been fired from less than two and a half meters away, Caña insisted, although there is nothing in Dr. Mendoza's report to indicate this. The real killers were "the same group (Will) was accompanying." In the state prosecutor's scenario, the order of the shots was reversed: first Brad had been shot in the side in the street and then *rematado* (finished off) with a slug to the heart on the way to the hospital in Gualberto's *vochito*.

The prosecutor's plot was immediately challenged by the APPO. "The killers are those who are shown in the film," Florentino López, the Assembly's main spokesperson, asserted at a meeting that night. But the order of the bullets and from how far away they were fired could now only be determined by the exhumation of Brad's body. And there was no body—he had been cremated the week before.

In at least two other killings of APPO members and/or teachers, Lizbeth had used this same ruse. According to the prosecutor, José Luis Colmenares, who was shot August 10 by a police sharpshooter as he marched through the city, had been murdered during an altercation with his *compañeros* about public urination.

Lizbeth Caña collaborated closely with Secretary of Citizen Protection Lino Celaya. Both reported to Ulises's secretary of government Heliodoro Díaz who in turn reported directly to URO. There seems little doubt that the state prosecutor's accusations of murder against Brad's comrades came straight from the top to divert attention and silence the growing clamor for justice.

Despite her science fiction scenario, the (now ex-) state prosecutor was right on target on one score. Brad Will's murder did "internationalize" the conflict. Only hours after Will was killed, U.S. Ambassador Garza green-lighted President Vicente Fox to send in the troops.

A few days before Mexico's new president, Felipe Calderón, was to be inaugurated, on November 25, the Federal Preventative Police crushed a last desperate APPO mega march, brutally beating and arresting 141 citizens and flying them a thousand kilometers north to another state where they were imprisoned and systematically tortured, according to abundant testimony collected by the International Civil Commission for the Observation of Human Rights (CCIODH), a largely European group of independent investigators who visited Oaxaca from December 2006 through February 2007.

The repression that day forced the APPO into a defensive posture, trying to raise bail and secure the release of its prisoners. The city quieted. The streets were swept clean and the walls whitewashed to blank out all evidence of the seven-month-long uprising.

Then, on November 28, in keeping with this whitewash, as expected, *El Chino* and Manuel Aguilar were released from custody because of "insufficient evidence" by Judge Vittoriano Barroso, with the stipulation that they could not be re-arrested without the presentation of new evidence.

Dr. Luis Mendoza is otherwise occupied when I stop by CEMEFO, the Oaxaca city morgue, to ask him for a copy of the autopsy report upon which the state of Oaxaca has based its allegations. The coroner's identification of the bullets he extracted from Brad Will's body as 9 mm slugs is questioned by Miguel Ángel de los Santos, the Will family attorney. "Will died eight months ago," Mendoza complains testily, "do you know how many others have died since? How many autopsies I've performed?" He gestures to the morgue room where the cadavers are piled up.

The coroner is hunched over his desk, filling out the paperwork for one of the stiffs. He doesn't have any time to look for the autopsy report. I am not the first reporter to ask him about the document. "What paper are you from anyway?" he asks suspiciously and when I show him my press card he tells me that it doesn't sound like a real paper to him. "I know what I'm doing. I worked as a coroner in your country," he snaps defensively and waves me out of the office.

But Dr. Mendoza might not be quite as cocksure as he sounds. A top agent for the U.S. government in Oaxaca, who asks not to be named in this article, reports that Mendoza confided to him that he was no ballistics expert nor could he determine from how far away the bullets were fired.

I walk into the police commissary under the first-floor stairs of the Santa Lucía del Camino Municipal Palace. The small room is crowded with cops and cigarette smoke. Three of the officers are in full battle gear and the rest are all plainclothes. I have been warned not to ask for Pedro Carmona, the most prominent white shirt in the front-page photo that ran the morning after Brad's murder in *El Universal*. Carmona, who is alleged to run drugs and provide protection for the local *cantinas*, is described as *prepotente*, i.e., a thug with an attitude, who is always packing.

Instead I ask the desk clerk if I could get a few minutes with security supervisor Abel Santiago Zarate and police commander Orlando Manuel

Aguilar Coello. For all I know, the two are sitting in the same room behind me. The desk clerk studies my card. "*¡Qué lástima!* (What a shame!)," he exclaims. The supervisor had just left and wouldn't be back until after six. The *comandante* is off today. When I call back after six, *El Chino* is still not available. Nor would he or Aguilar ever be available on the dozen or so occasions I called back.

What does any of this prove? Only that Brad's killers are back on the job with the Santa Lucía del Camino police department, ready to kill again. Mexican justice is crippled by such impunity. Killer cops sell their service to local *caciques* (political bosses) and go right back to work as if nothing happened after they've performed their murderous errands. Those who direct this mayhem from their desks in the state houses and municipal palaces—the "intellectual assassins" as they are termed—are never held accountable for their crimes.

In March 2007, Kathy and Howard Will and Brad's older brother and sister paid a sad, inconclusive visit to Oaxaca. They had hired Miguel Ángel, a crackerjack human rights lawyer who has often defended Zapatista communities in Chiapas. John Gibler would translate. The Wills, upper-middle-class Americans from upper-middle America, had little experience with the kind of evil that lurks inside the Mexican justice system and the trip was a traumatic, eye-opening experience.

The federal attorney general's office (PGR) had taken over the case from the state in December 2006, but rather than investigating police complicity and culpability, was pursuing Lizbeth Caña's dubious allegations blaming Brad's companions for the killing. Gustavo, Gualberto, Leonardo, and Miguel Cruz were summoned to give testimony with the Wills in attendance. But testifying was a risky venture as they could be charged with the murder at any moment. Nonetheless, out of respect for the family, the *compas* agreed to tell their story to the federal investigators.

In solidarity with Brad's family, they declared themselves on hunger strike on the steps of the PGR headquarters out near the airport. The vigil was immediately broken up by a phalanx of federal cops. During the hearing, the witnesses were repeatedly questioned about and asked to identify not the cops who appear on Brad's film but their own *compañeros*, some of whom were masked, on tape shot by Televisa. They refused.

When Miguel Ángel de los Santos accompanied the Wills to a meeting with Caña, she touted her investigation and promised them a copy of it. But she refused to allow the family to view Brad's Indymedia T-shirt and the two bullets taken from his body. They were under the control of Judge Barroso, the same judge who had cut loose the cops, she explained. Howard Will grew apoplectic at Caña's stonewalling. "'Hardy' flew off the handle," Kathy reported in a phone conversation when she returned to the U.S., "It was a good thing I was there to cool him off."

At press conferences, the Wills pushed for a real investigation not just into Brad's death but also for all of the victims of Ulises's death squads. Out of 26 cases total, only two—Brad's and that of a soldier who killed a civilian—remain open investigations. The rest languish in the cold-case files.

Despite the fact that Brad Will was a U.S. citizen who filmed his own murder, the United States Embassy quickly lost interest in the matter, issuing only a single press bulletin October 27, 2006, the night of his death. Three days later, Ambassador Garza would extend his travel advisory, citing Brad's "senseless death." On the six-month anniversary of Brad's murder, the diplomat penned an op-ed for *Milenio*, complaining that there had been no "concerted effort" on the part of the Mexican government to push the investigation forward. Bush's man in Mexico lamented that "a concerned voice had been silenced reporting an important story." He closed with a quotation from Thomas Jefferson about a free press.

Garza's op-ed is the last mention of Will in any embassy document. Meanwhile, Brad grows deader every day. One gets the impression that both the U.S. and Mexican governments are waiting for this case to grow so cold that no one will ever be able to revive it.

The U.S. State Department has a certain conflict of interest in trying to push freshman Mexican President Felipe Calderón to collar Brad's killers. Oaxaca was all about a political deal between Calderón's PAN and Ulises's PRI. Save URO's ass and the PRI would support the president's legislative package—indeed, the PRI's hundred votes in the lower house of congress guarantee Felipe the two-thirds majority he needs to alter the Mexican constitution.

And at the top of Calderón's legislative agenda is opening up PEMEX, the nationalized petroleum corporation expropriated from Anglo and American owners in 1938 and a patriotic symbol of Mexico's national revolution, to private investment, a gambit that requires constitutional amendment. I myself heard Calderón make this pledge to privatize PEMEX to the American Chamber of Commerce before he was elected. Months after he had stolen the election from López Obrador, ex-Federal Reserve guru Alan Greenspan showed up in town to remind Calderón of his promise to privatize Mexican oil.

Washington, whose interests in Mexico Garza represents, is eager to see PEMEX privatized, an opportunity for Exxon and Halliburton (now PEMEX's largest subcontractor) to walk off with a big chunk of the world's ninth-largest oil company. Pushing President Calderón too hard to do justice for Brad Will could disaffect the PRI and put a kibosh on the deal.

It is not easy to imagine Brad Will as being a pawn in anyone's power game, but as the months tick by and the killing and the killers sink into the morass of memory, that is exactly what he has become.

****

Appendix A

John Ross's Published Works

BOOKS

Rebellion from the Roots: Indian Uprising in Chiapas (Common Courage Press: 1995) ISBN-10: 1567510426; ISBN-13: 978-1567510423

In Focus Mexico: A Guide to the Peoples, Politics, and Culture (Latin American Bureau, London 1996, 2nd edition, Interlink Pub Group Inc 2002) ISBN 1-899365-05-2; ISBN-10: 1566564212; ISBN-13: 978-1566564212

We Came To Play: Writings on Basketball, co-edited with Q.R. Hand (North Atlantic Books, 1996) ISBN-10: 1556431627; ISBN-13: 978-1556431623

The Annexation of Mexico: From the Aztecs to the IMF (Common Courage, 1998; Reprint edition, 2002) ISBN 1-56751-131-7; ISBN-10: 1567511309; ISBN-13: 978-1567511307

Tonatiuh's People: A Novel of the Mexican Cataclysm (Cinco Puntos Press, 1998) ISBN-10: 0938317415; ISBN-13: 978-0938317418

The War Against Oblivion: The Zapatista Chronicles 1994–2000 (Common Courage, 2002) [The Read & Resist Series] ISBN 1-56751-175-9; ISBN-10: 1567511740; ISBN-13: 978-1567511741

Murdered By Capitalism: 150 Years of Life and Death on the American Left (Nation Books, 2004) ISBN-10: 1560255781; ISBN-13: 978-1560255789

Zapatistas! Making Another World Possible: Chronicles of Resistance 2000–2006 (Nation Books, 2006) ISBN-10: 1560258748; ISBN-13: 978-1560258742

The History of Latin America: A Novella (Unpublished, 2007)
IraqiGirl: Diary of a Teenage Girl in Iraq, co-edited with Elizabeth Wrigley-Field (Haymarket Books, 2009) ISBN-10: 1931859736; ISBN-13: 978-1931859738
El Monstruo: Dread and Redemption in Mexico City (Nation Books, 2009) ISBN-10: 1568584245; ISBN-13: 978-1568584249

POETRY CHAPBOOKS

Jam: A Random Walk (Mercury Litho-Bug Press: 1976)
12 Songs of Love and Ecocide (1977)
The Psoriasis of Heartbreak (1979)
The Daily Planet (1981)
Running Out of Coastlines (1983)
Heading South (1986)
Whose Bones (1990)
JazzMexico (Calaca de Pelón: 1997)
Against Amnesia (Calaca de Pelón: 2002)
Bomba! (Calaca de Pelón: 2006)

ANTHOLOGIZED IN:

Nuclear California (Sierra Club, 1984)
Third World Ha Ha Ha! (City Lights, 1995)
Forces for Change (Latinamerica Press 1999)
The Zapatista Reader (Nation Books, 2002)
Puro Border (Cinco Puntos, 2003)
Shock & Awe (Creative Arts, 2003)

John Ross's articles have appeared in numerous publications and news outlets, including CounterPunch, the *San Francisco Bay Guardian*, Pacific News Service, the *Nation*, the *Progressive*, and *La Jornada*. His commentaries and observations can also be found on the Internet at: www.johnross-rebeljournalist.com.

Appendix B

Links and Resources for Independent Journalists

Written and compiled by journalist and radio producer Catherine Komp, with additional material researched and compiled by Laura Brickman.

PART 1: RADIO JOURNALISM TOOLS

Spend a couple days or weeks getting familiar with recording equipment and digital editing software. If your local community station offers an equipment and training program, take advantage of it to practice and become familiar with what's available. If you're thinking about doing radio journalism on a regular basis, consider investing in your own equipment. A lot of radio journalists produce broadcast quality material using the following:

Basics and Equipment

- Recorder: Zoom H2 or H4. Both have broadcast quality built-in mics; the latter has an XLR line-in, which provides more flexibility in various recording environments. Tascam also makes several affordable portable recorder models for field interviewing. A few sites that have competitive prices for digital recorders: *www.amazon.com*; *www.bswusa.com*; *www.bhphotovideo.com*
- Digital editing: Audacity is a free, open-source digital editing program that works on PC, Mac, and Linux computers: *http://audacity.sourceforge.net*

- Transom.org is an excellent resource for many things radio, and also conducts in-depth equipment reviews and regularly updates its equipment guides:
- Gear Guides: *http://transom.org/topics/tools/*
- How-to's: *http://transom.org/topics/techniques/*
- The Knight Digital Media Center also provides a number of tutorials on equipment: *http://multimedia.journalism.berkeley.edu/tutorials/#audio*
- J-Lab has a great overview on what to include in your field recording kit and how to record in the field:
- *http://j-learning.org/present-it/audio/how-to-record-audio-for-the-web/*

Eventually, you might want to expand your equipment to include some more advanced items:

- Additional external mics, such as a shotgun mic to gather sound from a distance.
- A more advanced digital editing program, such as Adobe Audition, now available as a Cloud product (*https://creative.adobe.com/products/audition*) or Reaper (*www.reaper.fm*).
- Mobile digital editing, such as Hindenburg: *http://hindenburgsystems.com*
- An expanded home studio: *http://transom.org/2012/small-recording-studio-update/*

Get familiar with how your equipment works before you conduct your first recordings. Practice with your friends, roommates, family, and colleagues. Pay attention to microphone placement, background sounds, and what you're hearing through your headphones. Make adjustments in order to get the best possible recording. Ideally, you always want the mic to be about an apple's width from the speaker's mouth.

http://j-learning.org/present-it/audio/how-to-record-audio-for-the-web/
This article from J-Lab is a great starting point for a reporter new to field recording. It outlines the basics for collecting a good piece of audio and lists the equipment you'll need, what to do with it, and how much you can expect to spend.

www.bswusa.com
BSW, or Broadcast Supply Worldwide, is a specialized retailer, and the slight up-tick in price compared with distributors like Amazon is worth it. You can call the company and reach a knowledgeable salesperson who can walk you through product specifications, recommend items based on need, and offer a price cheaper than what is listed on the website.

www.bhphotovideo.com
B&H Photo, Video, and Pro-Audio also offers competitively priced equipment. The company has an extensive selection, and each item is accompanied by a list of product highlights and customer reviews.

http://transom.org/2012/small-recording-studio-update/
This is a useful primer by Jeff Towne on how to set up a home recording studio. He goes through each component you'll need to make a decent recording—microphones, hard drives, and so on, describing the basic use for such tools and then recommending equipment packages.

http://transom.org/topics/tools/
Transom's Gear Guide is a running list of equipment and software reviews and some detailed how-to's for editing, mixing, recording, and interviewing.

www.radioactive.org.uk
Provides equipment, training and technical assistance for community radio stations, recording studios, and radio training centres in the UK and around the world.

Editing and Mixing

http://transom.org/topics/techniques/
Transom's how-to's on editing, mixing, recording, and interviewing are a valuable resource for producing your own radio story. Posts address many of the common challenges radio journalists encounter, so try searching the site for the problem you're grappling with.

http://multimedia.journalism.berkeley.edu/tutorials/#audio
The UC Berkeley Graduate School of Journalism is another good resource to skim for sound editing tutorials on a variety of software platforms, recommendations for field equipment, and general structural lessons for producing an effective story.

www.hindenburgsystems.com
Hindenburg's Premium audio editing software is intended for journalists and podcasters, and is an all-in-one program for producing audio. Check it out. It has a downloadable 30-day trial for free.

www.mediabistro.com/10000words/12-useful-online-tools-for-journal-ists_b144

Twelve useful tools for online journalists offers some excellent tips for incorporating technology into successful reporting. Each tip includes a link to a related online service.

PART 2: FIELD RECORDINGS AND INTERVIEWS

Now that you're familiar with your equipment, it's time to put it to use. Spend a couple of months conducting field recordings and interviews, and editing those down to stand-alone segments (Q&As, vox pops, segments of speeches).

- Practice recording in different environments: one-on-one interviews, speeches, round-table discussions, outdoor and ambient sound. If you're recording at a formal event, you'll want to request credentials and permission to record. Also, find out recording logistics. Will there be a "mult-box" to plug into? Is there another way to plug into the PA system? If there is no PA system, can put your recorder on a podium? At big events, where there are speakers and an audience, you should avoid recording from a distance (unless you have a shotgun mic). A handheld recorder will not capture broadcast-quality sound from even short distances away from the speaker's mouth. If you're recording outside, you'll want to have a windscreen. If you're recording in a home or office, you might want to use a mixer, to get both your voice and your subject's voice recorded. If you're doing person-on-the-street interviews, make sure you hold the mic (don't let the interviewee hold it) and keep it as steady as possible (as you're practicing, you'll hear how often slight movements of mic and recorder will be picked up on the recording). If you are getting a lot of "handling noise" from your mic, try wrapping it with a small section of rubber garden hose slit lengthwise.
- Throughout recording, wear headphones so you can monitor what your recorder is capturing. Pay attention to your levels, which should fall between 6dB and 12dB. Overmodulated sound cannot be fixed post-production, so make sure you're not recording "too hot."
- If possible, take notes while you are recording to indicate time points and identify sections of the recording you'd like to use. This will help you when you return from your field recording or interview, especially if you need to quickly pull audio for a timely project or production. Depending on how you're using your audio, you may want to log all of your tape (a rough transcript with time codes). Logging tape is particularly useful when producing a "hard news" reporter feature or long-format documen-

tary. Also, come up with a system for archiving your recordings. There may be opportunities in the future to go back to that interview and re-use the audio, for example if you interview a prominent person who later passes away, or when doing a "Year in Review" segment.

Interviewing

www.mediacollege.com/journalism/interviews/questions.html
This is a short, comprehensive guide on interview prep from the Media College, "a free resource for film and digital media production." Some seemingly obvious points, such as the usefulness of researching your subject and preparing interview questions, are kindly reiterated. There are some less obvious tips here, too.

www.ijnet.org/stories/5-interview-tips-every-journalist-needs
Here's a list of tips for effective interview prep, conducting, and review. It's concise and full of links to related articles.

www.rfi.fr/talentplusen/articles/066/article_129.asp
This article from Radio France International explains that preparing for an interview starts with identifying a goal. Interviews fall into categories and should be prepared and conducted with an objective in mind. The article also includes some helpful tricks of the trade and interview techniques.

News gathering/reporting

http://www.theguardian.com/science/blog/2011/jan/19/manifesto-simple-scribe-commandments-journalists
Former *Guardian* science editor, letters editor, arts editor, and literary editor Tim Radford has condensed his journalistic experience into a handy set of rules for aspiring hacks.

www.radiodiaries.org/diy-radio
The *Teen Reporter Handbook* is written for youth but has some great tips for anyone new to journalism. You can read the whole thing online or download a free PDF.

www.newseum.org/digital-classroom/video/getting-it-right/default.aspx
This page from the Newseum Digital Classroom discusses mistakes in journalism, how they occur, and how they can be prevented. You need to create an account to view the video called "Getting it right."

www.poynter.org/category/how-tos/

Poynter's Newsgathering and Storytelling how-to's discuss a variety of topics useful for journalists and aspiring writers. You'll find posts on issues both topical and trade related.

http://billgentile.com/backpackjournalism/

Award-winning veteran journalist and producer Bill Gentile maintains the Backpack Journalism Blog to define, discuss and promote backpack journalism. The site won the "Best Site for Journalists" award in 2012. Bill also offers online video-journalism workshops.

Tools

https://medium.com/@Journalism2ls/75-tools-for-investigative-journalists-7df8b151db35

Here is a catalogue of more than 75 tools for investigative journalists from @Journalism2ls. Tools included in the catalogue provide support for news monitoring, social media, data collection, story mapping, and production, among other things.

www.boomeranggmail.com

You can use boomerang to schedule emails to be sent at a later time. It works very well with gmail, not as well with some other email clients.

www.rapportive.com

Rapportive is a free plug-in that you can use to link contact info to your email account.

http://docs.google.com

Use Google Docs to write and share documents, and collaborate with other gmail users.

www.evernote.com

Evernote is a digital filing cabinet that stores clipped web content for later reading on multiple devices.

www.workflowy.com

Workflowy is a simple list-making tool. Organize your to-do lists and access them from anywhere.

www.skitch.com

With this screen-shot utility you can add text, graphics, and annotations. (It's helpful for mapping, too.)

www.instapaper.com
You can use instapaper to save articles from your browser to read later when offline.

Using Skype for Interviews and Broadcast

http://ijnet.org/en/blog/best-apps-and-tools-recording-phone-or-skype-interviews
Recent list of apps and tools for recording phone and Skype interviews.

http://deepdishwavesofchange.org/node/2402
Tips for setup to use Skype to broadcast interviews.

http://www.ifree-recorder.com
Windows platform free recording software for Skype-records your voice on one channel and the caller's on the other. Can be set to start automatically.

www.macworld.co.uk/how-to/mac-software/how-record-skype-video-calls-on-mac-3525900
For recording from Skype on Mac computers.

Online Storage and File Transfers

www.dropbox.com
Dropbox is an online backup device allowing users to share and organize big and small files.

www.backupify.com
Backupify is cloud back-up service especially useful for businesses, schools, and other organizations. It handily links directly with Google apps and backs up content once a day.

www.wetransfer.com
You can use We-transfer to send up to 2 GB of data directly to a friend's email account for free. Larger files can be transferred with a paid account. It works very well over slow international Internet connections.

www.transferbigfiles.com
As the name suggests, you can use Transfer Big Files to share files up to 20 GB and multiple files with multiple people. You must first create an account. It also offers a service to add "chat" features to a website.

Apps for Android and iOS phones

http://dispatchapp.wpengine.com
Dispatch is an app that allows you to upload material instantly to Tumblr. It was developed as part of a research project conducted by Stanford and Columbia and is intended to allow journalists working in conflict areas to publish their work securely and anonymously.

Additional useful apps:

http://appadvice.com/applists/show/apps-for-the-mobile-journalist
www.journaliststoolbox.org/archive/mobile-journalism
www.rjionline.org/news/7-most-useful-apps-mobile-journalism
www.journalism.co.uk/news/20-tools-and-apps-for-digital-journalists/s2/
    a554321
www.journalism.co.uk/news/10-useful-ios-apps-for-mobile-journalism/
    s2/a557539
http://wannabehacks.co.uk/2014/05/23/the-must-have-apps-for-journal-
    ists-as-voted-by-the-wannabe-hacks-community/

PART 3: THE CRAFT

After you're comfortable with the basics of recording and editing, start focusing on interviewing, news gathering, writing, reporting, and on-air delivery skills. Lots of online resources are available, and there are often free webinars that you can sign up for or find archived (*Ijnet.org*, linked below, lists some of them). As you're studying tips and formats, listen critically to other radio producers, dissecting how they've put together programs and reports. When you're ready to produce your own segment or report, give yourself an assignment. Write a "nut graph" that boils down the story into one or two paragraphs. Include a list of sources (both interviews and primary source materials) and estimated length of the segment or report.

Start with straightforward projects using one to three sources and build up to more complex ones. Share your work with others and ask for critical feedback. Journalism is a lifelong education, and you'll grow, improve, and learn new tricks along the way.

Writing and Delivery

www.newslab.org/resources/voicetip2.htm
Voice coach Ann Utterback offers some tips for improving vocal delivery. Breathe properly, speak conversationally, and try not to get sick.

www.ijnet.org/video/breathing-broadcast

Here's a video, also featuring Ann Utterback, from the International Journalists Network. She discusses how many people breathe ineffectively and teaches the viewer the abdominal/diaphragmatic breathing method, which allows for full, healthy breath and is most conducive to clear and effective speech.

www.mervinblock.com/?q=node/29

News guru Mervin Block provides some great tips for news writing. He'll tell you that the best stories are short and straightforward.

www.newscript.com

New Script is an online guide for radio writing techniques. It's a great resource for journalists new to the field.

www.ehow.com/how_7843639_write-radio-news-story.html

This article on how to write a news story expands on four fundamental points: Keep the listener in mind; determine the length of your story; write as you speak; and focus on the five W's (Who, What, When, Where, Why).

http://www.theguardian.com/science/blog/2011/jan/19/manifesto-simple-scribe-commandments-journalists

Former *Guardian* science editor Tim Radford has 25 commandments for journalists and those hoping to become journalists. In one sentence: write for your reader.

www.suite101.com/article/writing-for-news-radio-a62727

"How to Write for News Radio" from Suite 101 provides some interesting formatting tips for radio scripts. They should be double-spaced and written in all caps. Acronyms that are spelled out should be written with dashes (e.g. NATO vs. N-C-A-A), and pronunciation guides should be provided.

www.ehow.com/how_4840290_write-radio-news-broadcasts.html

Here are 10 tips from e-How on writing scripts for radio news (you'll begin to notice some of the same points coming up again and again).

www.homeworktips.about.com/od/paperassignments/a/How-To-Write-A-News-Article.htm

Here's About.com's take on writing a news article. It's fairly brief and includes links to related articles.

www.makeuseof.com/tag/5-free-writin-style-guides-online

Includes a link to The Yahoo! Style Guide which is no longer available online, but can be purchased in book form. Also has style guides from the BBC and Guardian newspaper in London, as well as the famous guide by Strunk & White.

https://en.wikipedia.org/wiki/News_style

Wikipedia has a more encyclopedic discussion of news style that discusses the field's nuance and terminology in depth.

http://bsideradio.org/learn/writing-a-radio-script/

Here are some tips from B-Side on writing a script for a radio feature story. The article gives you a step-by-step guide on the writing process and includes some aesthetic tips as well as a sample script.

http://bsideradio.org/writing-for-radio-some-new-thoughts/#more-288

Tamara Keith, a reporter and host on NPR, discusses some of her own techniques for putting her ideas on paper and adapting what she has written for the radio. Above all, she says, write the way you speak.

http://transom.org/2006/nancy-updike/

Here's an interesting thread from Nancy Updike, a producer for "This American Life" and other programs on NPR. It starts with an essay about writing quality stories for the radio, but make sure to read the thread as well. The comments from readers and Nancy's responses are as informative as her original piece.

Ethics and Standards

www.spj.org/ethicscode.asp

The Society of Professional Journalists (SPJ) asserts that a journalist's primary objective should be to forward public enlightenment. This code of ethics details the journalist's responsibility to seek truth and report it, minimize harm, act independently, and be accountable.

www.taoofjournalism.org

The Tao of Journalism builds its ethics on the principles of transparency, accountability, and openness and includes a pledge journalists can sign and display to demonstrate their commitment to ethical journalism.

http://americanpressassociation.com/principles-of-journalism/
The Statement of Shared Purpose from the Project for Excellence in Journalism (PEJ) outlines nine journalistic principles identified after extensive surveys, public forums, and research in the field.

Archives and Resources for Research

http://ijnet.org/en/blog/10-google-tools-investigative-reporters-can-use-find-information
From the International Journalists' Network—a guide to googling more effectively.

www.journaliststoolbox.org
The Journalist's Toolbox is an archive of content presented by the Society of Professional Journalists. The categorized index is an excellent resource for conducting research.

www.journaliststoolbox.org/archive/broadcast-journalism
The archive of links from the Journalist's Toolbox is worth browsing. It's a diverse collection of helpful websites and articles (kind of like this appendix).

www.independentreports.net/links.html
Here's another list of useful links from Independent Reports, a resource for community media.

www.indytech.org/page3.html
IndyTech is another website with a collection of resources related to community media, and this page will link you to manuals and training resources from various community radio outlets.

www.quotationspage.com/search.php3
Quotations Page is a search engine for finding quote sources and authors. You can type all or part of a quote to find who said it and when.

http://reporter.asu.edu
Here's "A Journalist's Guide to the Internet" from the Walter Cronkite School of Journalism and Mass Communication at Arizona State University. It includes links to government databases, business directories, non-profit records, and so on. It's all useful information for a reporter investigating a story.

www.nreisner.com/FindingAlmostAnybody.htm

This guide to finding information on an individual for a story might be slightly outdated (there's an article discussing methods for gaining access to records in filing cabinets and phone books) but it's still interesting, if just for a historical perspective.

https://www.cia.gov/library/publications/resources/the-world-factbook/index.html

Here's the World Factbook from the CIA. The CIA knows all (or so they tell us).

www.quora.com

Quora is a question-and-answer-style social media platform. You can browse curated and filtered information from all of the site's users or link to your Facebook account.

http://archive-research.com

Archival Research is a service specializing in locating, copying, and digitizing archived historical records in all media for a variety of clients. The company's work ranges from simply finding and copying a few pages of records to long-term research projects. It conducts research to find the archival records that respond to your request, will digitally scan or photograph them, and can often deliver them to you within 24 hours.

www.reporterslab.org/fact-checking-grows-in-latin-america

This article from Reporters Lab discussing the emergence of fact-checking sites in Latin America includes links to different fact-checking outlets in the region.

http://africacheck.org

A site similar to the above, recently created for Africa by the French AFP Foundation.

Helpful Organizations

www.airmedia.org

Association of Independents in Radio (AIR) is an online network of producers, stations, and networks. You can become a member and join the online community.

www.prx.org

Public Radio Exchange (PRX) is public radio's largest distribution marketplace. You can publish and license your own content, or buy pieces for local air.

www.nwu.org

National Writer's Union (NWU) is the only labor union for freelance writers. It has 1,200 members and 13 chapters. You can join up and pay your dues.

www.spj.org

The Society of Professional Journalists calls itself the nation's most broad-based journalism organization, dedicated to encouraging the free practice of journalism and stimulating high standards of ethical behavior. It was founded in 1909.

www.thirdcoastfestival.org

Third Coast Festival is an audio library, weekly radio show, and podcast based in Chicago. It hosts annual competitions, curates audio stories, and shares them for free.

www.radio4all.net

A-Infos Radio Project "Radio for All" is a grassroots group that also curates content and shares it for free. Its goal is "to support and expand the movement for democratic communications worldwide." The group exists to serve as "an alternative to the corporate and government media which do not serve struggles for liberty, justice and peace, nor enable the free expression of creativity."

www.archive.org

The Internet Archive is a non-profit providing access to an online library of digitized content. It's a huge and diverse collection of audio, video, and text.

www.radio-info.com

Radio Info, the trade publication for the music radio industry, is an online community as well as a resource for information.

Social Services for Collaborating

www.storify.com
    With Storify, you can create and publish your own narrative using content from online media.

www.flavors.me
    Flavors helps you create a branded personal web presence by combining various social media platforms into one URL.

www.hootsuite.com
    Hoot Suite is a tool for managing social media that allows you to work with multiple networking sites simultaneously. It's particularly useful for organizations tracking a large online presence.

http://findings.com
    Browse quotes from various platforms, collect them, and share them online. You can view based on genre and popularity or search a field or phrase of interest.

https://delicious.com
    "Delicious" is the oldest social shared bookmarking community. You can keep lists of your own private weblinks, or share them with your friends.

www.ifttt.com
    With Ifttt (pronounced like "gift") you can create online triggers called recipes that allow you to prompt certain actions in an "if...then..." format. (Like: "IF I'm tagged in a Facebook photo THEN upload that photo to my Dropbox.")

****

If you have additional tips or links (or updates to these), please feel free to e-mail them to: tips@rebelreporting.com.

Notes

FOREWORD

1. *Papers of Thomas Jefferson*, vol. 11: 48—49, http://press-pubs.uchicago.edu/founders/print_documents/amendI_speechs8.html.

2. John Nichols and Robert W. McChesney, *Tragedy and Farce: How the American Media Sell Wars, Spin Elections and Destroy Democracy* (New York: The New Press, 2005).

3. Ben Scott, "Labor's New Deal for Journalism: The Newspaper Guild in the 1930s," PhD dissertation, University of Illinois at Urbana-Champaign, 2009, ch. 7.

4. The two classic works are: Walter Lippmann, *Liberty and the News* (Princeton: Princeton University Press, 2008); Walter Lippmann and Charles Merz, "A Test of the News," *The New Republic*, August 4, 1920.

5. See John Nichols and Robert McChesney, "Bush's War on the Press," *The Nation*, December 5, 2005.

6. Chris Hedges, *Empire of Illusion* (New York: Nation Books, 2009), p. 170.

7. For a long discussion of the reliance on official sources and other problems built into the professional code for journalism, see Robert W. McChesney, *The Problem of the Media* (New York: Monthly Review Press, 2004), ch. 2, ch. 3.

8. For a variety of treatments of this issue, see Howard Friel and Richard A. Falk, *The Paper of Record: How the New York Times Misreports U.S. Foreign Policy* (New York: Verso, 2004); Edward S. Herman and Noam Chomsky, *Manufacturing Consent* (New York: Pantheon, 1989); Jonathan Mermin, *Debating War and Peace: Media Coverage of U.S. Intervention in the Post-Vietnam Era* (Princeton University Press, 1999).

9. For a superb treatment of this issue, see W. Lance Bennett, Regina G. Lawrence and Steven Livingston, *When the Press Fails: Political Power and the News Media from Iraq to Katrina* (New York: Cambridge University Press, 2007).

HANDING IT DOWN: FOUR LECTURES ON REBEL JOURNALISM

1. Paraphrased from the book, in Italian, *Il cinico non è adatto a questo mestiere* ("*A Cynic wouldn't Suit This Profession: Conversations about Good Journalism*") available at: http://edizionieo.it/catalogo_visualizza.php?Id=865

LECTURE ONE

1. Josh Wolf was imprisoned for a total of 226 days for failing to reveal his sources.

2. Former Ambassador Joseph C. Wilson IV had gone to Niger to investigate claims of the purchase of uranium by Saddam Hussein for Iraq's nuclear weapons program. When he found no truth to these assertions and wrote a July 2003 op-ed for the *New York Times* stating so, he became the victim of a smear campaign by Bush administration officials, which included a leak to the press that his wife, Valerie Plame, was a C.I.A operative. Eventually, Vice Presidential aide Lewis "Scooter" Libby (the accused leaker) was found guilty of perjury in March 2007, but President George W. Bush commuted his prison sentence in July 2007.

3. Biographies of I.F. Stone include Andrew Patner, *I. F. Stone: A Portrait* (New York: Pantheon,1988) and D. D. Guttenplan, *American Radical: The Life and Times of I. F. Stone* (New York: Farrar, Straus and Giroux, 2009). Stone collected his own writings in numerous volumes, including *The I. F. Stone's Weekly Reader* (New York: Random House, 1973), a collection of articles from his weekly publication (1953-1971), the contents of which can also be found online here: www.ifstone.org/weekly_searchable.php

4. The largest of the Nazi concentration camps, it was liberated on April 29, 1945.

5. From *Zapatistas! Making Another World Possible: Chronicles of Resistance 2000-2006* by John Ross (Nation Books, 2006).

6. From the poem "*Como Tú*" by Roque Dalton, 1975.

7. The poem "*Como Tú*" by Roque Dalton, 1975, translated by John Ross, used by permission.

LECTURE TWO

1. A published version of this poem is available here: www.revistadelauniversidad .unam.mx/8210/leon/82leon.html, together with a video of the author. Used with permission of Dr. Miguel León-Portilla.

2. FY2010 figures show that "If Wal-Mart were a country, its revenues would make it on par with the GDP of the 25th largest economy in the world by surpassing 157 smaller countries." More information available at: www.businessinsider.com/25-corporations-bigger-tan-countries-2011-6?op=1

3. As of January 2014, there were over 2,000 retail units in Mexico. http://corporate .wal-mart.com/our-story/locations/mexico

4. See http://carnegieendowment.org/files/nafta1.pdf

5. According to the 2009 report *Humanitarian Crisis: Migrant Deaths at the U.S.-Mexico Border*. See www.aclu.org/sites/default/files/pdfs/immigrants/humanitariancrisisreport.pdf

6. The original article is not available online, but Ross recounts the story in a May, 1994 article for the publication *Lies of Our Times* which is republished here: http://flag .blackened.net/revolt/mexico/comment/media94.html

7. A Mayan rain deity.

LECTURE THREE

1. A Zapatista political initiative designed to link the Zapatistas with other pre-existing resistance groups throughout Mexico in the months leading up to the presidential elections of July 2006.

2. See more in Part II of this book, "Who Killed Brad Will?"

3. For more on this history, see www.cnn.com/TRANSCRIPTS/0607/17/lt.02.html

4. From *Murdered By Capitalism: 150 Years of Life and Death on the American Left.* Copyright © May 27, 2004 John Ross. Reprinted by permission of Nation Books, a member of the Perseus Group.

5. More on the history of the "Gulf of Tonkin Incident" is available here: http://www.counterpunch.org/2014/08/05/robert-s-mcnamara-and-the-real-tonkin-gulf-deception/ ,and here: http://fair.org/media-beat-column/30-year-anniversary-tonkin-gulf-lie-launched-vietnam-war/

6. Annual report for the year 2006 can be found here: http://en.rsf.org/press-freedom-barometer-journalists-killed.html?annee=2006

7. According to the Committee to Protect Journalists, in 2006, Iraq was by far the most dangerous country in the world for reporters. You can view the statistics sorted by year or by country here: http://cpj.org/killed

8. According to the independent human rights organization Freedom House.

9. Thirty-one had been killed as of early 2015 - see http://cpj.org/killed/americas/mexico

10. From the U.S. invasion in March 2003 up to 2009, 140 reporters have died in Iraq. Of those, 89 were murdered and 50 were said to have been killed in crossfire. The majority, 117, were Iraqi. As might be expected 128 were men. The toll included 36 photojournalists, 85 reporters and editors, 9 producers, and 7 technicians.

11. An updated total from the Committee to Protect Journalists states that from 2003 to 2009, 105 reporter deaths were due to insurgency and other armed action groups. Seven were embedded reporters. The United States had killed 14 news gathers during this time period.

12. "The Colonel," from *The Country Between Us* by Carolyn Forché, © 1981 by Carolyn Forché. Originally appeared in Women's International Resource Exchange. Used by Permission of HarperCollins Publishers.

13. See the book *IraqiGirl: Diary of a Teenage Girl in Iraq*, edited by Elizabeth Wrigley-Field and John Ross available from www.haymarketbooks.org/pb/IraqiGirl

14. On December 22, 1997, at least 45 members of the pacifist group *Las Abejas* were murdered in the community of Acteal. *Las Abejas* were sympathetic to the Zapatista forces, but were not members of the Zapatistas. The attack has been blamed on paramilitary forces, but there are also accusations of Mexican government support for the paramilitary groups. More information available at: www2.gwu.edu/~nsarchiv/NSAEBB/NSAEBB283

LECTURE FOUR

1. For the full story, see http://www.counterpunch.org/2007/01/17/vibrant-as-the-paint-on-the-walls/

2. Votan Zapata is a legendary manifestation of the spirit of Emiliano Zapata honored by members of the Zapatista Army of National Liberation.

3. For more, see: *Zapatistas! Making Another World Possible: Chronicles of Resistance 2000-2006* (Nation Books, 2006), p.245

4. On December 22, 1997, at least 45 members of the pacifist group *Las Abejas* were murdered in the community of Acteal. *Las Abejas* were sympathetic to the Zapatista forces, but were not members of the Zapatistas. The attack has been blamed on paramilitary forces, but there are also accusations of Mexican government support for the paramilitary groups. More information available at: www2.gwu.edu/~nsarchiv/NSAEBB/NSAEBB283.

5. from "*Como Tú*" by Roque Dalton, 1975, translated by John Ross, used by permission.

WHO KILLED BRAD WILL?

1. This quotation ("*somos un ejército de soñadores y, por lo mismo, somos invencibles*") originated in an exchange of letters between Zapatista Subcomandte Marcos and Uruguayan

journalist and novelist Eduardo Galeano. The letters were printed in Mexico's daily newspaper *La Jornada* (July 4, 1994), and appear in their original form on the official EZLN website here: http://palabra.ezln.org.mx/comunicados/1994/1994.htm. The English translation of this phrase has appeared on over one hundred websites and printed newsletters as a symbol of the Zapatista spirit.

2. For more on Hakim Bey and his writings, see: http://hermetic.com/bey

3. The Ruckus Society first began offering direct-action training to environmental and anti-globalization activists in 1995. For more information, see: www.ruckus.org

4. A reference to the 1975 novel *The Monkey Wrench Gang* by the late Edward Abbey, which was an inspiration to the radical environmental activist group Earth First! and others. Earlier traditions of "monkey-wrenching" date back to the Industrial Workers of the World "sabocat" and the 15th-century Belgian workers who would throw their wooden shoes (called *sabots*) into the gears of the textile looms in a protest against industrial automation.

5. Food Not Bombs began in the 1980s as an anti-nuclear activist organization dedicated to non-violent social change. Today they have hundreds of chapters around the United States and the world, regularly providing free vegetarian food in an effort to combat war and poverty. Many Food Not Bombs activists have been arrested and prosecuted for giving free food to homeless residents of San Francisco and other cities.

6. The ABC news report and Brad Will's response are discussed in this article from 2004: http://gaycitynews.nyc/gcn_339/protestersallegepolice.html

7. The full text of Gibler's report can be found here: http://nova.wpunj.edu/newpolitics/issue42/Gibler42.htm. John Gibler later wrote *Mexico Unconquered*, a book about social movements in Mexico struggling against corruption and violence: www.citylights.com/book/?GCOI=87286100093700

8. One of many articles around the globe describing the immense size of the demonstrations can be found here: www.smh.com.au/news/world/12m-now-thats-a-protest/2006/07/31/1154198065627.html

9. Jill Friedberg's excellent independent film *Un Poquito de Tanta Verdad* (A Little Bit of So Much Truth) tells the story of the takeover of 14 radio stations and a TV station during the protests in Oaxaca. More information is available at: www.corrugate.org/un-poquito-de-tanta-verdad.html

10. Following massive protests, a partial recount of votes was ordered. The results of this partial recount, still favoring Calderón were announced on August 28, and the new president was inaugurated on December 1st.

11. The most famous photograph of Che Guevara after he was killed in Bolivia on October 9, 1967, shows him lying on his back, shirtless, with his pant legs pulled up to his knees.

Index

About the Author

In his lifetime John Ross published ten volumes of fiction and nonfiction and numerous books of poetry. He was the recipient of the American Book Award in 1995 and the Upton Sinclair prize in 2005. After tearing up his draft card in 1957, Ross moved to Mexico, where he published his first article. After that he went on to write for the *San Francisco Bay Guardian*, *Noticias Aliadas*, *La Jornada*, *Counterpunch*, *Alternet*, and many others.

ABOUT THE EDITORS

Cristalyne Bell is a freelance journalist and activist with experience in print, radio and video journalism. She grew up in Arkansas and attended Madison College, where she served as Editor for *The Clarion*, winning several awards. While a journalism student at Madison College, she attended two lectures by visiting author John Ross—it was an experience that inspired her and changed her life. Cristalyne has volunteered at WORT-FM Community Radio in Madison, covering both national and international issues, and previously worked with documentary filmmaker Sam Mayfield. She continues in her passion for traveling, storytelling, and social justice.

Norman Stockwell serves as WORT Radio's Operations Coordinator. He has been working at the station in music and news programming since 1983. He has hosted programs of "A Public Affair" since 1989, covering such issues as the murder of the Jesuits in El Salvador, the Gulf War and its aftermath, the pro-democracy movement in Nepal, and the Zapatista uprising in Chiapas, Mexico. He has also covered the WTO meetings in Seattle and Cancún, the FTAA meetings in Miami, the Democratic Conventions in 1996, 2000, 2008, and 2012, the Republican Conventions in 2004, 2008, and 2012, the spring 2004 and 2009 presidential elections in El Salvador, Mexican presidential elections of 1988 and 2006, and the November 2013 presidential election in Honduras. He coordinated community radio coverage at the World Social Forum in Porto Alegre in 2002, 2003 and 2005; the Polycentric Forum in Caracas, Venezuela, in 2006; the WSF in Nairobi 2007, Belém in 2009, Dakar in 2011, and Tunis in 2013 and 2015; and the US Social Forums in Atlanta and Detroit. He also coordinated the IraqJournal website in 2002-2003. In 2011, he regularly reported on protests in Madison for Iran's PressTV and other outlets. His reports and interviews have appeared on Free Speech Radio News, DemocracyNow!, and AirAmerica, and in print in *Z Magazine*, the *Capital Times*, *AlterNet, Toward Freedom*, the *Tico Times*, and elsewhere.

Copyediting by Elizabeth Bell.
Index prepared by Jillian Potter.

Lightning Source UK Ltd.
Milton Keynes UK
UKOW03f0329290417
300171UK00001B/7/P